Who Am I to Judge?

Who Am I to Judge?

Responding to Relativism with Logic and Love

By Edward Sri

Ignatius Press
San Francisco

Augustine Institute
Greenwood Village, CO

Ignatius Press Distribution
P.O. Box 1339
Fort Collins, CO 80522
Tel: (800) 651-1531
www.ignatius.com

Augustine Institute
6160 S. Syracuse Way, Suite 310
Greenwood Village, CO 80111
Tel: (866) 767-3155
www.augustineinstitute.org

Cover Design: Enrique J. Aguilar Pinto

ISBN: 978-1-62164-165-0

Library of Congress Control Number 2016955378

Printed in Canada

To my daughter Elinor

Contents

Preface

Sixty-five college students every Monday, Wednesday, and Friday. Most of them don't want to be there. How do I present the Christian moral tradition in a way that is captivating and compelling to these young people—especially when so many of them think of morality as a bunch of arbitrary rules from religion, assume each individual should be free to make up his own morality, and balk at the slightest hint that someone might be trying to tell them what to do?

This is what I was pondering while preparing to teach a course called "Christian Moral Life" at a small Catholic college in Kansas many years ago.

I understood where they were coming from, for I had been there myself at one time. When starting college, I had many questions about Catholic moral teachings regarding life, sex, and marriage. And the secular environment on campus regularly challenged traditional moral values. Anyone daring to claim that some behavior was morally right or wrong was typically accused of being judgmental and intolerant: "Who do Christians think they are to tell other people how to live? Don't judge others just because they have different values and different lifestyles. Don't impose *your* morality on me!" In the face of such opposition, I was not always sure how to respond.

Over time, thankfully, through good friends, mentors, teachers, priests, and books, I eventually came to see more clearly the beauty of the Catholic moral vision. It makes sense out of life. It points to what makes us truly happy. It shows us the pathway to virtue, friendship, and lasting love. It also encourages us to face the truth about ourselves—our faults, our weaknesses, our sins—in light of the truth about God's unwavering love for us. It thus leads us to a profound encounter with Christ's mercy and to a power that enables us to live and love in a way we could never do on our own: the power of God's grace. Indeed, the Christian moral life is the pathway to human flourishing. Only by living the way God intended for us, by living in union with Christ, can our hearts' deepest desires be fulfilled.

But that's not the average person's impression of Catholic morality and certainly not that of the majority of college students I was preparing to teach. Most had been shaped by the culture's individualistic outlook on life and came with the presupposition of moral relativism. For them, morality was just personal opinion. Each individual makes up his own truth. Each decides for himself what is right or wrong. The one really bad thing to do in life is to make a judgment about someone else's moral beliefs. That would be intolerant.

Much of this book draws on years of teaching about the problem of moral relativism to college students and young adults throughout the country. I am thankful to so many of them for their sincere questions and honest dialogue about the moral issues they face. Countless insights from those conversations have, no doubt, left their mark on the pages of this book. I am also thankful for the many young people of all sorts of backgrounds—Catholic, Protestant, non-Christian, agnostic, and even atheist—who were open to an alternative way of looking at life, very different from what the secular, relativistic world offers and whose lives were significantly changed as a result. I pray that this short, simple work may touch your life as well, as it introduces some key features of a Catholic moral worldview and offers practical keys for talking about morality with your relativistic friends.

Edward Sri
October 22, 2016
Memorial of Pope St. John Paul II

PART ONE

THE CHALLENGE

Chapter One

A New Kind of Intolerance

"So how did you respond to that question about gay marriage?"

That's the simple question Kara was asked by a friend on the way out of class her freshman year at college. She was taking a political science course at a big state university when her professor passed out a survey about moral beliefs and politics. One of the questions was about gay marriage.

"I said I was against it," she said.

Kara grew up in a Catholic family, went to youth group as a teenager, and continued practicing her faith in college, going to Mass every Sunday on campus. Her faith was important to her, and she held traditional values about marriage and family.

"Well, I said I was for it!" her friend replied.

Unlike Kara, he believed each individual should be free to make up his own morality and decide for himself what marriage is. But he shrugged off Kara's seemingly antiquated beliefs and went his way, saying, "To each his own. ... See you at the party tonight!" Despite the difference of opinion, all seemed to remain peaceful between the two friends—until Kara showed up at the party.

As soon as she entered the room, her friend stood up and shouted to get everyone's attention. "Hey, everybody! ... Guess what Kara said about gay marriage in class today? She said she was *against* it! Can you believe that? She's against gay marriage!"

Suddenly, Kara found herself on trial, surrounded by dozens of her peers berating her: "How could you say that?" "Who are *you* to decide what marriage is for everyone else?" "Why are you so intolerant? ... You shouldn't impose your views on other people." She tried to explain her position. But it only made things worse. Some even called her a bigot and a "gay hater." In the end, the only thing she could do was walk away and leave.

Devastated, Kara left that party changed. She had never taken such a thrashing for her faith before. She pondered whether it was worth it all. "I don't know if I want to stand up for my beliefs like this again," she told herself. "It costs way too much."

> She still held the same moral convictions about abortion, marriage, and sex, but with a new, two-word qualification: "For me."

Understandably, Kara wanted to fit in, be accepted, and be liked by her friends. "But I learned that day," she later reflected, "that if I stand up for what I believe, I would suffer a lot for it. And I didn't think I had it in me to take another beating like that again." That's when Kara started becoming a relativist—at least in her heart. At first, the change was subtle. She still held the same moral convictions about abortion, marriage, and sex, but with a new, two-word qualification: "For me." When hot-button moral issues would come up in conversation, she would say to her friends, "Well, *for me* abortion is wrong. ... I would never have an abortion. But if other people think abortion is okay, that's fine for them." Or: "*For me* marriage is between a man and a woman, but if someone else thinks differently, then that's okay for them, if that's what makes them happy."

Those two little words, however, marked a big change in Kara's mindset. No longer did she uphold a real right or wrong in the world, a moral standard that applies to everyone. Rather, she relegated morality to a matter of personal taste, like someone's favorite color, type of music, or ice cream flavor. "For me, abortion is wrong" became just like "For me, chocolate is better than vanilla."

But here's the problem with this two-word qualification: once we make that subtle move—once we give up on the existence of moral truth in the universe—then anything goes, anything is morally justifiable, and anything is possible. And not just for other people, but for ourselves as well. Without a moral structure, we are more likely to compromise when faced with our own temptations. But should this really trouble us? After all, people change their preferences in music, food, drink, and sports. So if morality is just personal taste, then why shouldn't our moral beliefs and practices change over time, too?

That's what started happening with Kara. Surrounded by a decadent culture on her college campus and peers who were living very different kinds of lifestyles than she, Kara started to waver. If there is no real right or wrong, if everything is just a matter of personal taste, then maybe it's not a big deal if I try *X* or do *Y*? Over time, Kara found herself making compromises in her own moral life, doing things she never imagined herself doing. She started skipping Mass on Sunday, and, by the end of her freshman year, she had stopped practicing her faith altogether and had fully espoused moral relativism. Kara's experience is a true story (though her name has been changed here) and one that exemplifies the challenges of relativism today.

No Safe Environment

Every age has had its bullies who shame or oppress people because of race, religion, color, or gender. We should always fight against bigotry of this sort and treat all people with dignity, even if they are different from us or we disagree with them. But today we experience a new kind of bullying. It's what Joseph Ratzinger (now Pope Emeritus Benedict XVI) called the "dictatorship of relativism."[1] Relativism is the idea that there is no truth, that each individual decides for himself what is true and what is right and wrong. A relativist would say that all truth claims are subjective, merely reflecting one's personal feelings, opinions, or desires. You can have *your* truth, and I can have *my* truth, but there is no *the* truth to which we are all accountable.

> "For me, abortion is wrong" became just like "For me, chocolate is better than vanilla."

"Today, having a clear faith based on the Creed of the Church is often labeled as fundamentalism," Ratzinger said. "Whereas relativism ... seems the only attitude that is acceptable in modern times."[2] Indeed, the person who is *not* a relativist is often not tolerated in society. The pro-life woman, for example, who says that abortion is wrong is likely to be called "judgmental"; someone who says that marriage is between a man and woman will be labeled "intolerant";

---

[1]   Joseph Cardinal Ratzinger, Homily, Mass for the Election of the Supreme Pontiff, St. Peter's Basilica, April 18, 2005, http://www.vatican.va/gpII/documents/homily-pro-eligendo-pontifice_20050418_en.html.

[2]   Ibid.

the Christian college student who says that premarital sex is wrong will be mocked and brushed aside as being "rigid" or "out-of-touch."

In this way, the relativistic culture tends to marginalize those who hold traditional moral convictions. Since these views do not fit into the relativistic worldview, Christians holding to them are likely to be stereotyped, shamed, and ostracized just as Kara was. As Ratzinger noted, relativism is emerging as a new kind of totalitarianism—one which seeks to push the Christian belief in truth further out of the mainstream. In his words, "We are building a dictatorship of relativism that does not recognize anything as definitive and whose ultimate goal consists solely of one's own ego and desires."[3]

In this environment, many good people feel paralyzed. They sense that there are real rights and wrongs in the universe—that some things are immoral for anyone to do— but they are not sure what to say or are afraid to voice their convictions. Many young adults and college students say they have experienced something like Kara did—maybe not as intensely and maybe over a different issue, but with the same result: they walk away feeling shamed for their beliefs. And even those who have not faced such hostility directly have seen what happens to others and fear they might be next. They are afraid that they will be misunderstood or rejected by their coworkers, family, and friends, so they keep silent, hiding their convictions—which is exactly what the relativistic culture wants.

Others wonder whether making moral judgments is itself a problem, maybe even the chief problem in the world. Sociologist Christian Smith explains that this is a common mindset among young adults today. For many of them,

---

[3] Ibid.

"Morality is ultimately a matter of personal opinion. It is wrong to render moral judgments of the moral beliefs and behaviors of other people—unless they directly harm you. Everyone should tolerate everyone else, take care of their own business, and hopefully get along."[4] This attitude characterizes even many Christians who point out that Jesus said, "Do not judge."

Some fear that it is actually the people who believe in moral truth who cause all the bigotry, hatred, and violence in the world. In their eyes, claims to absolute moral truth led to evils such as the Holocaust, the Rwandan genocide, and 9/11. Who wants that? Isn't it better to just let everyone believe whatever they want and coexist?

Smith, however, shows a serious shortcoming with this perspective:

> At the same time, these emerging adults have not been taught well how to differentiate between strong moral and religious claims that should be tolerated, if not respected, and those that deserve to be refuted, rejected, and opposed. Very few have been given the reasoning tools and skills to discern such important differences. As a result, many emerging adults simply end up trying to completely avoid making any strong moral claims themselves, as well as avoiding criticizing the moral views of others . . . *But what few of them seem to realize is that such a position makes it impossible to rationally evaluate or criticize any moral wrong, including the horrific destruction and violence that helped drive them to this tolerant position in the first place. That is a problem.*[5]

This is the challenge that we will address in this book: How do we talk about morality in an age that no longer believes in moral truth? If anyone making a claim to truth is viewed

---

[4] Christian Smith, *Lost in Transition: The Dark Side of Emerging Adulthood* (New York: Oxford University Press, 2011), 26.

[5] Ibid., 26-27. Emphasis added.

as an intolerant bigot, then how do we even begin to speak about some actions being wrong all the time? After all, who wants to be perceived as a mean, judgmental person? If I live in constant fear that I might be shamed for my moral convictions, then maybe it's just better to keep quiet.

This short, highly readable book is meant to help you rise above the mainstream "anything goes" attitudes around you and give you greater clarity and confidence in talking about morality with relativistic friends—greater clarity about how to think with a classical moral worldview and greater confidence in sharing that beautiful vision with others. I am convinced that the more we are immersed in a proper moral vision, the more effective we will be in responding to the relativistic mindset.

This book also offers seven practical keys you can use in your conversations with relativists. These are not proofs, but tools for you to have on hand—like keys in your pocket—to use over time in your conversations when appropriate. These key attitudes and approaches can help you open the door to moral truth in the lives of your friends. With a firm foundation in a classical moral vision and practical keys to engage the culture of relativism—and with the help of God's grace—may this book help equip you to radiate God's moral truth with great courage and love.

Questions for Reflection/Discussion

1. Have you ever felt afraid to bring up a moral topic or talk about a moral issue with your friends or family? Why were you afraid? What were you afraid of?

2. Joseph Ratzinger was quoted as saying, "Today, having a clear faith based on the Creed of the Church

is often labeled as fundamentalism." Do you think that's true? Explain.

3. Have you ever been labeled "judgmental" or "intolerant" by others just because of your moral beliefs? Perhaps by a friend, teacher, relative, or group you were involved with? If so, share a story about what happened.

4. What can you do differently so that you are not afraid to talk about moral truth with others?

5. Many people today think that groups who believe in truth are the ones who cause all the problems in the world—such as 9/11, the Rwandan genocide, etc.—so they think it's better never to make moral judgments about other people's actions and to just tolerate each other. What's the problem with this approach? (See the quotation in this chapter from sociologist Christian Smith.)

Chapter Two

Clashing Worldviews

I will never forget the first time I heard the words "moral relativism." I was in college, having a discussion with a friend who was taking an ethics class that semester. He told me the professor promoted moral relativism—the notion that there is no objective moral truth and no right or wrong. "Truth is relative," my friend said. "What's true for you may not be true for other people. There's no absolute objective truth that applies to everyone, so each individual makes up his own morality."

I had not yet studied much philosophy or theology, but what he was saying didn't sound right. I started asking him questions: "So you believe in relativism? You really believe that there is no absolute truth ... no truth that applies to everyone?"

"Yes."

"Is *that* true?" I asked.

"Yes."

"So, is *relativism* true? Is it absolutely true, true for everyone, that there are no absolute truths?"

Silence.

Then I went for the kill, "Well ... your relativism seems logically inconsistent!"

"*Gotcha!*" I thought to myself. I was quite proud of my amateur apologetic moves. My friend had no answer. He even laughed and admitted that, in espousing relativism, he was asserting at least one truth: that there is no truth. He acknowledged that his position was not consistent.

But he did not change his mind. I might have won the argument on that particular point, but he continued being a relativist. And he was not too worried about how intellectually sound his position was. Relativism just felt right: We shouldn't tell other people how to live. Individuals should decide for themselves what is right and wrong. Each person has the freedom to live however he or she wants. We shouldn't impose our morality on other people. My friend was quite content to continue in his relativistic outlook on life despite the arguments presented to him. And many people in our culture are likely to do the same.

> I eventually became convinced that merely debating a relativist does not work.

No Quick Fix

After several experiences like this one with my friend throughout the years, I eventually became convinced that merely *debating* a relativist does not work. Relativism is not something that can easily be overthrown with a quick, three-point apologetic argument or a superficial "Top Ten" list of reasons why it's wrong. It's part of a worldview deeply engrained in the souls and lifestyles of countless men and women. Like my friend from college, many people today hold relativistic attitudes not so much because they have a clearly thought out philosophy of life, but rather because their relativistic tendencies are rooted in various assumptions they have absorbed from the culture and in the habits of thinking and living they have formed over a lifetime. Most people's relativistic perspectives are simply based on unquestioned presuppositions. "Of course, relativism is right. ... Why? ... Well, because each person should decide for himself what is right and wrong. No one person, group, or religion can tell others how to live. Judging other people is bad."

To respond effectively to relativism, we have to go deeper. We need to step back and consider an entirely different way of looking at life, what one could call a classical moral worldview. Though it has been around for over two millennia guiding countless individuals and shaping whole cultures, this vision for life is new to most people today, even to many Christians. It has not been handed on effectively and, in many ways, has been suppressed in the modern age. This vision draws on the way ancient pre-Christian writers such as Homer, Aristotle, and Plato understood the good life, and it is shaped by what Jesus, the Bible, and the Church have taught throughout the centuries. If we want to effectively engage the relativistic culture around us, getting a better grasp of this moral vision is crucial for three reasons.

First, many Christians themselves do not understand the key features of a classical outlook on ethics. We tend to think about morality primarily as rules—hoops we have to jump through to obey God, to be a "good person," and to eventually get to Heaven. If we don't understand our own moral tradition well, how are we going to be effective in communicating it to others? One of the reasons relativism is so prevalent today may be that we Christians have not done a good job of explaining the Christian moral vision. Instead, we have left people with the impression that morality is just about random rules from our religion that we're trying to impose on other people.

Second, we must recognize there is no quick fix to the problem of moral relativism. There's no elevator speech that dispels all relativistic tendencies in an instant. Because relativism is so ingrained in people's lives, we must invest ourselves for the long term as we accompany people in life. Understanding the classical view of morality is essential if we're going to expose the many shortcomings of relativism, bring out its negative effects in people's lives, and offer them an alternative way to think about moral matters.

Third, and most importantly, there's a certain persuasiveness that comes when we encounter the inner coherence of the classical moral vision. As we will see, when all the pieces—virtue, friendship, freedom, happiness, love—come together in our own lives, they resonate with people's experiences and shed light on what they hope for in life. And this may do more to move someone closer to accepting moral truth than an argument about why relativism is logically inconsistent. This approach appeals not only to their minds, but also to their hearts—to their felt need for love, friendship, community—and directly relates to what they're going through day to day.

The Real $100 Bill

When government agents are trained to identify counterfeit currency, they begin by studying authentic money. After they have spent countless hours touching, tilting, looking at, and looking through genuine bills, detectives will be more likely to notice a false one. Similarly, the more we grasp and internalize a Catholic outlook on morality—and the more our minds and hearts are shaped by God's beautiful plan for the moral life—the more we will be able to detect and diagnose the various counterfeit approaches to life offered by our secular relativistic world. Formation in a classical moral vison will do more to combat relativism than shallow arguments for why relativism is wrong.

So I invite you, next, to step back and consider a way of looking at life that's very different from what the mainstream culture offers. While this classical moral vision draws upon the Christian tradition, you don't need to be a Christian to appreciate it. Most of what we'll discuss is readily accessible to people of all faith traditions, lifestyles, and backgrounds, as well as to people who do not believe in

> We have left people with the impression that morality is just about random rules.

God. And whatever background you may be from, you don't have to accept this vision. But you should at least be open-minded enough to try to comprehend it on its own terms, if for nothing else than to understand where Christians are coming from when they talk about moral truth.

However, I'm confident that if you are open to hearing about this classical view of morality, and "try it on," so to speak, you will find that it fits rather nicely. It makes sense. It makes sense out of our lives and sheds light on our experiences. It relates to what we most deeply hope for in life.

Questions for Reflection/Discussion

1. The author told a story about proving to his friend that relativism was logically inconsistent. Explain that point in your own words: Why is it illogical for relativists to say there is no truth?

2. How successful was this approach in convincing his friend that relativism was wrong? Explain.

3. Have you ever tried to convince a friend relativism is wrong? What was your approach? How well did it go?

4. Why does the author say it's not effective merely to debate with relativists? What must we do instead?

5. The best way to detect counterfeit money is to study authentic currency. And the same is true with morality. What can you do to form yourself more with an authentic, Catholic moral worldview?

PART TWO

A NEW VISION

Chapter Three

"But I'm Not Hurting Anyone!"

Imagine a businessman, married for fifteen years, father of two children, successful in his career, known for his volunteering in the community, and well-liked by his friends. One day, he travels by plane across the country for work. Sitting next to him on the plane is an attractive woman, and they hit it off, sharing a nice conversation on the flight. At the baggage claim, he discovers they're staying at the same hotel in town, so they ride together in the shuttle. After check-in, they stop to have a couple drinks together in the hotel lobby. At the end of the evening, she invites him to her room. *What should he do?* Many people believe that he should say no. But why?

"Because he's a married man."

"So?"

"If he goes to her room, he may want to sleep with her."

"And what's the problem with that?"

"He's married! He shouldn't be sleeping with someone who's not his spouse!"

"Well, that might be what *you* think. But what if *he* views things differently? What if for him it's not a big deal to sleep just one time with another woman?"

"But he made a vow. He'd be breaking a promise to his wife."

"Have you ever broken a promise before? Are you perfect in all your promise-keeping? Have you ever said you'd do something but failed to do it? Who are you to judge?"

"But this is marriage."

"Look. He's been faithful for fifteen straight years. What's one simple night compared to thousands of nights of marital fidelity?"

"It's just wrong … even if it's only one night."

"How can you say that? I don't understand why you're so hung up on what this man chooses to do in his private life. That's his business, not yours. Maybe you would never cheat on your spouse—and that's fine for you—but many other people do this all the time. You shouldn't impose your views on him. He's free to do whatever he wants with his life."

"But it's a sin."

"Sin? … What? … Oh … I see now … That's a Christian word. You must be one of those judgmental Christians always looking down on other people. Let me be clear. This businessman is *not* a Christian, so that should settle things. You as a Christian can go on and believe in the 'sacredness of marriage'—and that's fine for you. But this man is not a Christian. Please don't force him to live by your religious standards."

"But marriage isn't just a religious thing. It's an institution that society depends upon. If you don't have strong marriages, you won't have strong families and you won't have a good society."

"But that's just it—this man *has* a fine marriage. He and his wife are happy together. We're talking just one night with another woman. He's not hurting anyone!"

"He's hurting his wife."

"But she will never know about it."

"He's hurting the woman."

"No. She's a consenting adult. She can make her own decisions. And besides, she's the one who invited him. If anything, he'd be hurting her if he turned down the invitation."

"Well, he's hurting himself."

"I don't see how."

"He's not being true to himself."

"How do you know that? If he is attracted to her and desires to sleep with her, it seems like he's being very true to himself. He might be hurting himself if he *didn't* take advantage of the opportunity."

"But he'll feel guilty about it later."

"There you go again using another Christian word. Guilt. You Christians are obsessed with guilt. My motto is 'No regrets.' I want to live life to its fullest. Why waste time second guessing our decisions and worrying about guilt?"

"I once heard a speaker explain that sex is not just about pleasure. God ordered the sexual act toward the procreation and education of children. And you can't separate the unitive and procreative aspects of the sexual act. Sex should be an expression of love that is total, exclusive, free, and fruitful. That's what Theology of the Body teaches … "

Yawn. "I'm not really sure what you're talking about. But it's clear you're getting religious on me again. Let's just agree to disagree. If you think sex should only be in marriage that's fine for you … if that's what makes you happy. I respect that. But please don't impose your views on others. If the businessman wants to sleep with that woman at the hotel, that's fine for him. That's his choice. It's his life. He's not hurting anyone."

The Questions Behind the Questions

It's hard to talk about morality in our relativistic culture. When the person you're having a conversation with doesn't believe in truth or any real right or wrong in the universe, there's not much common ground for dialogue. Every time you try to explain why something is immoral, you find yourself feeling unsure of how to make the case ("I have no idea how to explain this to this person!"). You feel humiliated ("They think I'm insane."). You feel labeled ("They think I'm just some religious fanatic."). You might even feel shamed as they criticize you for being judgmental or intolerant. Whatever you're saying is definitely not working and only seems to be making things worse. It's as if you are speaking a completely different language than your friend.

If we're going to be successful in our conversations with relativists, we have to ask the question *behind* the question. Underneath the objections "Who are you to judge?" or "Why are you so intolerant?" are deeper questions about life that many in our age never take time to consider. And these fundamental questions point to how we can engage moral relativism more effectively. Step back with me now as we consider one of those crucial questions: In what does happiness consist?

Funeral

Imagine it's your funeral. You've lived a long life, and the people closest to you gather to pay their final respects. Some of them will stand up to say a few words. Picture·those loved ones walking up to a podium—your spouse, children, siblings, friends, colleagues, and neighbors. One by one, they speak about your life and what they appreciated most about you. What would you want them to say?

When asked how they want to be remembered most, people typically give two kinds of responses.

First, they tend to mention various noble *qualities*: they want to be remembered for being loyal, kind, generous, joyful, hard-working, courageous, caring, loving, honest, selfless ... they want to be remembered as the kind of person who made an impact.

Second, people also tend to describe the *relationships* that are important to them: they hope to be remembered as a good friend, a good husband or wife, a good father or mother, a good colleague ... someone who made a difference in other people's lives.

Practically no one, however, says he hopes to be appreciated for being wealthy, powerful, or famous. Imagine a friend standing up at the funeral and saying, "Bob was a great guy ... He had *so much money!* The amount of savings he had in his bank accounts was just astounding. What an amazing man Bob was!"

Similarly, no one ever says he hopes to be known principally for his career. "Bob was an outstanding sales manager. Over 10 years, he helped expand the company's market share by 9.7%. The company sold more corn flakes than ever under Bob's leadership."

Neither do people mention popularity as the chief quality for which they want to be remembered. "Bob was so famous. He had so many friends following him on social media. ... And do you remember that picture he posted last year—he got 50,000 likes in just a few hours. Wasn't Bob such a great man?"

Pondering this defining moment, the moment we will be remembered by our closest relatives and friends, cuts through the many activities, pursuits, pressures, and preoccupations that fill up our daily lives. It helps us get to the heart of what really matters most. And while there is nothing wrong with having a great career, money, influence, fame, or fun, most of us, when we stop to think about it, realize that there is more to life than all this. These aren't the most important qualities we want our lives to be defined by. Instead, when we think about what makes a wonderful life, we tend to focus on our closest relationships and the qualities (the virtues) that go along with living those relationships well. And this shouldn't surprise us. For having good, fulfilling relationships is at the heart of what life is all about.

Ethikos

Take a moment right now and think about what you consider to be three of the most important moral issues we face today. You can put the book down and write them out, if you'd like, or simply come up with a short list in your head. You might list topics such as the environment, political corruption, corporate greed, or lack of respect for people of all races, religions, and walks of life. Or you might think of poverty, immigration, or war. Or, still, you might mention human life issues, such as abortion or capital punishment, or matters related to sexuality, such as divorce, contraception, and the definition of marriage.

Whatever your background, whether you consider yourself progressive or traditional, the list you came up with probably reflects a *modern* view of ethics—one that is not very personal and that doesn't often touch on our daily actions. Think about it: How much do questions about global warming, medical testing on animals, or physician-assisted suicide really affect the choices I make every day—the way I treat my spouse and kids, the way I interact with my friends and colleagues, how hard I work, how well I face adversity, or how well I serve those in need?

We tend to think of ethics primarily as the big issues "out there" in the world: problems in the culture or topics to be debated in the public square. These topics may be matters for the United Nations or the United States Congress to address, and governments may need to set up rules to protect individual rights and harmony in society. But for the most part, these issues don't direct how I live my life on an everyday basis. They come into play in those rare moments when I'm

> Practically *every moment is an ethical moment* because ethics is fundamentally about a person's character.

facing a moral dilemma that touches on those larger, more global issues: I'm thinking about throwing away a plastic bottle in the garbage can—will that hurt the environment? My marriage didn't turn out the way I expected, so I'm contemplating getting a divorce. My girlfriend got pregnant; is it okay if I help her get an abortion? What should we do in these situations? That's what we tend to think ethics is primarily about.

The classical view of ethics, however, is much bigger—and one that directly impacts our day-to-day lives. Certainly, thinking through good social, economic, and political structures is important. But the arena where ethics is primarily played out is not in the world of public policy and theory, but rather inside each person's heart, moment-to-moment.

In fact, the Greek word that philosophers such as Plato and Aristotle used to describe the drama of the moral life is *ethikos*, which means "pertaining to character." For them, ethics involved much more than an isolated ethical moment or rules that come into play when facing a certain moral situation. For them, practically *every moment is an ethical moment* because ethics is fundamentally about a person's character—the disposition to live a certain kind of life. Ultimately, ethics is intensely personal. It considers where a person's life is heading and what kind of person one is becoming. It's not merely about public policy, but how one treats the people in his daily life. In sum, ethics is not simply a question of *what*—"What should I do in this situation?"— but even more fundamentally, a question of *who*—"Who do I want to become?"

Begin with the End in Mind

That's why I like the funeral example so much. It helps us to think about where our lives are going. Who do I want to become? What kind of life do I want to live? These are questions about our *telos*—an important term I want to make sure you understand. *Telos* is the Greek word for end, purpose, or goal. We all want to be happy. But to achieve a happy, flourishing human life, we must first have clarity about what we're really aiming for. An archer can't hit the target if he doesn't see the bullseye. A soccer player can't score if he doesn't know where the goal is. A pilot can't complete his flight if he doesn't have a destination. And we, as human persons, can't live a successful life—a truly happy life—if we don't keep our *telos*, our purpose, in mind.

One thing that usually becomes clear in the funeral exercise is that the purpose of life does not consist in the things that most often allure us: wealth, power, pleasure, and fame. These will not make us happy. Deep down, we know we're made for something more. We long to have good *relationships*. We can have all the power, money, comfort, pleasure, and prestige in the world, but if we don't have anyone to share it with, we know we won't be happy. This tells us something about the purpose of a human life: our *telos* has something to do with friendship.

Indeed, this is the way God made us. He made us for relationships—friendship with him and with the people he has placed in our lives. Pre-Christian philosophers such as Plato and Aristotle understood that a happy life involves living one's relationships well. Similarly, Jesus taught that good relationships are at the heart of a good life. When someone asked him which commandment was the greatest, Jesus summed it up not legally but relationally: "You shall love the Lord your God with all your heart, and with all your soul, and with all your strength, and with all your mind; and your neighbor as yourself" (Lk 10:27). And from a Christian perspective, we are not made in the image and likeness of some vague higher power or impersonal spiritual force. We are made in the image and likeness of the God who exists as a profound unity of love, Father, Son, and Holy Spirit. God's inner life is all about self-giving love: the Father giving himself in love to the Son and the Son giving himself in

> We can't just wake up one morning and say, "I'm going to be an excellent friend," and suddenly expect to win Friend of the Year.

love to the Father, and the very outpouring of love between the Father and the Son is the Holy Spirit. Being created in the image and likeness of this Trinitarian God suggests that we're made to live like him—to live in relationship and to live a life of self-giving love. Written in the fabric of our being is this law of self-giving. This is what we're made for. Only when we give ourselves in love to God and others will we find our happiness.

So friendship with God and neighbor is what life is all about. That's why when we ponder the end of our lives, we tend to say we want to be remembered for what matters most: being a good neighbor, a good friend, a good sibling, a good spouse, a good parent, a good citizen, a good child of God. This is our *telos*, our end goal. A good life, a truly happy life, involves living those relationships with excellence.

But we can't expect to live our relationships well just because we want to. We can't just wake up one morning and say, "I'm going to be an excellent friend," and suddenly expect to win Friend of the Year. We need various qualities—qualities known as the virtues—that enable us to live our relationships with excellence. Any good friendship requires honesty, loyalty, generosity, joy, courage, self-control, perseverance, humility, and love. These are some of the virtues that enable us to live friendship well. Indeed, the virtues point us toward the kind of people we are meant to become: people who live their relationship with God and neighbor well. We can call this *man-as-he-could-be-if-he-fulfilled-his-telos*.

Most of us recognize, however, that we have areas where we fall short in virtue, areas where we could be better in the way we relate to others. We are not the best friend, spouse, parent, boyfriend/girlfriend, neighbor, or colleague we can be. We may have some noble qualities, but we also are fraught with various faults, weaknesses, bad habits, insecurities, fears about the future, and wounds from our past. And these keep us from experiencing the true joy and peace that comes from living our relationships well. All this is part of who we are right now: *man-as-he-happens-to-be*. We're a work in progress, hopefully moving in the right direction, but still on the way to our destination, our *telos*.

So here we see two key components: (A) *man-as-he-happens-to-be* and (B) *man-as-he-could-be-if-he-fulfilled-his-telos.*[6] Ethics is all about getting from A to B.

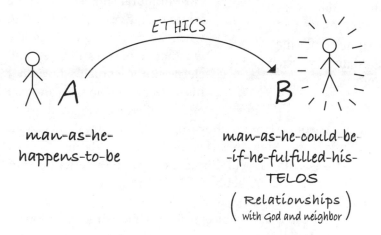

This background is helpful for engaging moral relativism. When talking with relativists, it's important to frame our individual choices in the larger context of our life story, instead of viewing them as isolated, random acts that have no meaning. If that were the case, it wouldn't matter what we choose to do with our lives. But in reality, our daily decisions—the way we treat our spouse, the way we work, what we watch, how we deal with adversity, how we talk about other people—should be seen within the narrative of our lives: where our lives are going and who we are becoming.

Our relativistic friends can always come up with some excuse or argument denying that something is wrong or justifying some action. But sometimes we need to break

---

[6]   See Alasdair MacIntyre, *After Virtue* (Notre Dame, IN: University of Notre Dame Press, 1981), 51-55.

through the webs of rationalization and simply ask the very personal question, "What kind of person do you want to become?" This helps frame one's current moral choices within the larger narrative of one's life. And when we do that, questions like whether a businessman should sleep with a woman who is not his wife are no longer abstract ethical dilemmas to be debated in a classroom. Nor are they isolated ethical moments about what you should do in this or that instance. Rather, the real question becomes: Will this act help you be a better person? A better spouse? A better friend? Will it help you live the kind of life you want to live?

> But is that the kind of person you want to become? That's the question relativism tends to avoid.

When we weigh our choices in light of those larger questions—in light of our *telos*—things become clearer. It helps us get to the heart of the matter quickly. Our individual choices really do matter. They lead us in one direction or another, either closer to the kind of person we want to be or farther away from that goal. Indeed, our actions forge our identity. For instance, one act of adultery makes you an unfaithful spouse. But is that the kind of person who you want to become? That's the question relativism tends to avoid.

"But I'm Not Hurting Anyone!"

Most people, however, are not *absolute* relativists. The average person probably would admit *some* things are wrong—things such as murder, stealing, rape, and kidnapping. We should avoid hurting other people. But when it comes to our private affairs, it's assumed everyone should be free to do whatever he wants with his life, as long as he's not harming others. There, in people's personal life choices, relativism should reign supreme. The underlying assumption here is that what we do in our personal lives does not affect other people. It is this modern supposition that we must now address.

C. S. Lewis, in his book *Mere Christianity*, described the human family as a fleet of ships sailing in formation. The voyage will be successful only if, first, the ships do not bump into each other, and second, each individual ship is running properly with its engines in good order. In this analogy he describes two key aspects of morality. Like the fleet of ships, we should avoid colliding into each other. This is the *first* aspect of morality, which focuses on social relations and safeguards fairness and harmony between individuals, communities, and nations. We should not murder, steal, cheat, rape, or enslave. We should avoid doing things that hurt other people. Most people today agree, at least to some degree, with this basic level of morality.

The *second* aspect of morality is what Lewis calls "the morality inside each individual."[7] This is like the seaworthiness of each individual ship. Just as each ship in the fleet must have its engines in good working order to ensure it does not crash into the other ships, so each person must have his soul running properly with virtuous behavior to ensure that he does not harm others.

People today are generally at ease with the first part of morality, the element of fair play in our social relationships. But many are not at all comfortable with the second aspect of morality, which focuses on the individual's life choices and moral character. Many think, "What I do in my private life is my own business. If what I'm doing doesn't hurt someone else, how can it possibly be wrong?" For example:

---

[7] C. S. Lewis, *Mere Christianity* (New York: Collier Books, 1960), 72.

"Who cares if I spend ten hours a day playing video games? What I do in my free time doesn't matter. If I want to play till 3 a.m. each day, that's my choice." Similarly, if a man wants to sleep with his girlfriend, what's the big deal? If she's a consenting adult, what can be the problem with that? If a millionaire doesn't give from his abundance to help those in need, or if an elderly person wants to end his life, these are their personal choices. And whatever they choose to do in their personal lives is right for them. Each person is free to do whatever he wants *as long as he's not hurting anyone.*

Lewis responds to this objection by returning to his fleet analogy. It's not enough to tell the ships, "Don't collide." And similarly it's not enough for society to say, "Don't hurt other people." If an individual ship's rudder isn't working, then it is not going to be able to sail properly or avoid crashing into other ships. And the same is true with people, as Lewis notes: "What is the good of telling the ships how to steer so as to avoid collisions if, in fact, they are such crazy old tubs that they cannot be steered at all? What is the good of drawing up, on paper, rules for social behaviour, if we know that, in fact, our greed, cowardice, ill temper, and self-conceit are going to prevent us from keeping them?" [8]

> If what I'm doing doesn't hurt someone else, how can it possibly be wrong?

The modern tendency to talk about social morality ("Don't hurt other people") while neglecting what Lewis calls "the morality inside each individual" is like commanding teenagers to obey the traffic laws without training them in the practical skills of actually driving a car. Imagine if all I did to prepare my teenage daughter to drive was hand her

---

[8] Ibid., 72.

the Department of Motor Vehicles handbook and have her
study it. Let's say I even had her memorize every rule of the
road. What would happen if I then handed her the keys and
said, "You can drive the car now. Just don't get into any
collisions"? How well do you think she would do? She might
know she is supposed to drive on the right side of the road,
stop at red lights, and never cross the double line. She might
know all the rules and even sincerely desire to follow them.
But that's not enough. If she has not been trained in the skills
of using the accelerator, touching the brake, and turning the
steering wheel, she is likely going to crash. Simply telling her
not to crash into other cars is not enough.

Similarly, unless individuals are trained in generosity in their
so-called private lives, they are going to do selfish things that
will hurt other people. Unless individuals are formed in courage
and taught to endure suffering for the sake of what is good,
they will do cowardly things that hurt other people. Unless
individuals are trained in chastity, sobriety, and other forms of
self-control, they will do out-of-control things that use and hurt
other people. Social harmony is built on the inner harmony of
individuals. A great society is built not just on good laws but
fundamentally on men and women of great moral character.
Or, as Lewis put it, "You cannot make men good by law: and
without good men you cannot have a good society."[9]

"And What I Have Failed to Do"

Whenever we encounter the myth that one's personal life
choices don't affect others, it's important to point out that
there are two ways to fail in life. We can fail morally by

---

[9]   Ibid., 72.

doing things that directly hurt others. But we also can fail by lacking in virtue, by not being the best we could be.

A prayer at Mass reflects these two aspects of human failure. When we confess our sins at the start of the liturgy, we express sorrow not just "…for what I have done" (the sins we have committed), but also "for what I have failed to do" (the good we did not do).

This reminds me that the way I live my life will affect others, for better or for worse. Though people often say they want to make a difference in the world, we must realize that *everyone* is going to do that. Everyone is going to leave their mark and have an impact on other people's lives. The question is whether it will be a good or a bad impact. Life is not all about me. It's not a solo game; it's more like a team sport, with our actions either benefiting or hurting the people in our lives. For example, I was never that great at basketball. I could follow the rules, but I was a poor shot, not very good at dribbling, and not much of a rebounder. When I played on the eighth grade "B" team, I stayed in bounds and avoided fouls, but I did not contribute much when I was on the court. My lack of ability hurt the team.

Similarly, it's not enough to go through life avoiding doing bad things that directly hurt other people. If I don't play the game of life with excellence, others will suffer the consequences. A father who spends too much time at work and not enough time with his children might not be hurting anyone directly in the sense of stealing from them or physically harming them. But his failure to invest personally in his children will deeply affect them, leaving a scar they will carry for the rest of their lives. His choices in his personal life are not simply private matters.

Similarly, the medical student who works only hard enough to pass will not be the best doctor she can be for her future patients. The man looking at pornography trains himself to treat women not as persons to love and respect, but as objects to be exploited for his own pleasure. The woman getting a divorce to run off with another man impacts not only her husband but also her children, who will be deeply affected by the broken home. We all make mistakes in life. And God is merciful and can bring healing

> The way I live my life will affect others, for better or for worse.

no matter what we've done. But to think that our choices each day in our so-called private lives don't affect other people is naïve. When we fail to be the best we can be, we have a negative impact on the people God has placed in our lives. Our spouse, children, friends, colleagues, employers, and parish will suffer from our lack of commitment and virtue, rather than being influenced positively. The great Roman orator Cicero once made a similar point:

> There are some also who, either from zeal in attending to their own business or through some sort of aversion to their fellow-men, claim that they are occupied solely with their own affairs, *without seeming to themselves to be doing anyone any injury.* But while they steer clear of the one kind of injustice, they fall into the other: they are *traitors to social life,* for they contribute to it none of their interest, none of their effort, none of their means.[10]

Cicero is pointing out the selfishness of anyone whose main goal in life is to do whatever he wants as long as he avoids hurting others. Is this the kind of people we want to be? The fact remains that we *will* hurt other people if we fail to give the best of ourselves at home, at work, at play, and in the world.

---

[10] Cicero, *De Officiis (On Duties)*, 1.29, in *Cicero: Complete Works*, trans. C. D. Yonge (Hastings: Delphi Classics, 2014) emphasis added.

Questions for Reflection/Discussion

1. Let's reflect on the funeral example mentioned in this chapter. Which qualities do you want to be remembered for most at your funeral? What does this tell us about what's most important in life and the kind of life you want to live?

2. We saw that ethics is about how to move from who we are right now to who we want to become—from *man-as-he-is* to *man-as-he-could-be-if-he-fulfilled-his-telos.* What is one area of your life that you think you need to work on most in order to become the kind of person God wants you to be? What is something practical you can do this week to help take a step closer toward becoming that person?

3. The chapter discussed two ways we hurt people: by directly harming them or by failing to be the best we can be for others. What are some ways we fail to be the best we can be? In our friendships? In our family? In our relationship with God?

4. Describe a time you personally hurt someone by failing to be the best you could be for them. Or think about this the other way around: describe a time you were hurt by someone who didn't harm you directly, but failed to be the best they could be for you.

5. What is one relationship you think God wants you to improve the most right now? What can you do practically to strengthen it?

Chapter Four

Friendship and Virtue

Imagine a culture that never breaks the Ten Commandments. No killing. No lying. No stealing. No coveting another person's spouse. Wouldn't that make it a great civilization?

Probably not.

Don't get me wrong. Avoiding violations of the Ten Commandments is certainly a good thing. Indeed, it would be a huge leap forward for most societies today. But to have merely avoiding hurting other people as the aim of one's life is not enough. We are made for something more. We are made for love.

Yet calling people to love is not something our secular world can easily do. If there's no truth, no real right or wrong, no purpose or *telos* in life, then the best we can come up with is tolerance. Let everyone do whatever they want as long as they don't hurt others. Respect other people's choices, don't judge their actions, and get a bumper sticker that says "coexist." That's what will make a great society.

But does that work well in real life? Is that what will make us happy? Imagine if someone asked me, "How's your marriage going?" and I replied, "My wife and I? ... We *tolerate* each other. ... We coexist." Would that be the ideal marriage?

Similarly, if someone asked me, "How's your family life?" and I said, "Oh, it's wonderful. We have a *great* family. We haven't stolen from each other, cheated on each other, or lied to each other. And we haven't even killed each other yet. We have such an amazing family!" No, a great family isn't one that merely avoids breaking the Ten Commandments. A great family is one that grows in unity, trust, care, and love.

Made for Friendship

Our hearts long not merely for tolerance; we yearn for love. Indeed, that's what we're made for—we are made in the image and likeness of the God who is love.

God is not some impersonal "higher power" or vague spiritual "force" like in *Star Wars*. No. He is a God who is madly in love with us. He created us freely out of love. He seeks us out when we turn away from him. He even became one of us and died on a cross for us so that we could be reunited with Him. God's very life is all about self-giving love, and he made us in his image to live like him. This is how we are wired. Written into our hearts is this law of self-giving: only when we live in imitation of the self-giving love of God will we find happiness and fulfillment in life.

> Our hearts long not merely for tolerance; we yearn for love.

As Pope St. John Paul II often said, "Man ... cannot fully find himself except through a sincere gift of himself." [11] Or, as Mother Teresa put it, "Unless a life is lived for others, it is not worthwhile." [12]

---

[11] Pope St. John Paul II, quoting Vatican II, *Gaudium et Spes* ("Pastoral Constitution on the Church in the Modern World"), 24.

[12] Michael Amoei, *Meeting Jesus in the Sacraments* (Notre Dame, IN: Ave Maria Press, 2010), 201.

Being respectful of others and steering clear of mistreating them is certainly important in any relationship, but it's just a starting point. It's not the end goal. It's not what brings us happiness. The real question in our relationships is not, "Do I avoid killing, stealing, cheating, lying, and disrespecting the people in my life?" but rather, "Do I have the ability to love them?"

Let's go back to the basketball example. If I were trying to convince you that I'm a great basketball player, you might ask what makes me so good. What would you think if I answered, "I'm a great basketball player because *I follow all the rules!* I stay in bounds. I don't double dribble. I don't travel with the ball. I should be in the NBA!" Certainly, following the rules of the game is important. But that's just permission to play. Unless I possess the *skills* of dribbling, passing, shooting, and defending, I'm not a good basketball player—no matter how carefully I follow the rules.

And the same is true in life. If we want to have good friendships and dating relationships; if we want to experience deep trust and intimacy in our marriages; if we want to build a strong family life for our children; if we want to love others truly—in sum, if we *want to live a happy life*—there is one thing we need that is critically indispensable and goes far beyond tolerance and coexistence. And that's virtue.

Let's zoom in now and take a closer look at one element of a classical moral worldview we touched on last chapter, the relationship between virtue and friendship:

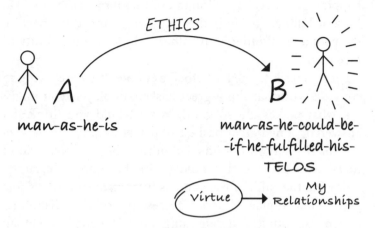

The *Catechism of the Catholic Church* defines virtue as "an habitual and firm disposition to do the good" (CCC 1803). It enables a man to "give the best of himself" to others. Think of virtue as a skill that enables one to love well—to love God and neighbor as if it were second nature.

But it's about much more than doing what's right every once in a while. There are three key characteristics exhibited in virtue. The virtuous person does the good *easily, consistently,* and *joyfully* (cf. CCC 1803–4). A PGA golfer, for example, can walk up to the tee, knowing exactly which club he is going to use, and take a good swing. He doesn't have to think much about it. It's *easy* for him. He *consistently* hits the ball where he wants it to go. And he experiences much *joy* in the game because he can play it well. An inexperienced golfer like me, however, might get lucky every now and then and hit the ball down the fairway. But that doesn't mean I possess the skill of a golfer. Most of the time, I'm putting the ball in the water, hitting a ground ball, or taking a swing and a miss. I'm far from consistent. And the sport is not second nature to me: I'm never sure which club to use, how to hold the club, and how much to bend the knees. I take dozens of practice swings and still never feel confident as I'm hitting the ball. It's not *easy* for me. And because I'm not a good golfer, there's usually not much *joy* when I play!

Like any sport or craft, our relationships also require many skills—the virtues—that enable us to do the good easily, consistently, and joyfully. My wife needs me to be thoughtful, not just on our anniversary, a holiday, or a date night. She needs me to get outside of my own world and think about her needs and the needs of our family all the time. Similarly, my kids need me to be kind to them every day throughout their lives, not just when I'm well-rested, relaxed, or in a good mood. My employer needs me to be responsible in seeing a task through from start to finish, not just when it's a project that interests me, but regularly out of service to the organization's mission. And my friends need me to be trustworthy when they share something confidential—not just occasionally but all the time. The virtues aren't simply good qualities that make us nice. Rather, they make us reliable, dependable, and trustworthy friends. They enable us to give the best of ourselves in our relationships.

Flying High

Since my childhood, I've been enthralled by flying. I loved going to the airport and seeing planes take off and come in for landing. And when onboard, I always wanted to sit by the window so that I could gaze at the sky above and look down at the clouds and the ground far below. To this day I still like to look out the window when traveling by plane because of how fascinated I am about being thirty-six thousand feet in the air.

Now, here's a question for you: After hearing of my passion for flying, would that ever make you want to get into an airplane with me in the cockpit? No way! I may value flying and have strong feelings about airplanes, but if I do not have the *skills* to fly a plane, you don't want to fly with me as your pilot!

Similarly, my father was a surgeon, and I grew up following him to the hospital and looking at books and pictures about anatomy and surgical procedures. I have fond memories of my dad as a doctor and continue to place surgeons in high esteem. However, would you want to get on the operating table with *me* as your surgeon just because I value surgery so much? Hardly. Since I never went to medical school and do not possess the *skills* to perform operations, you don't want me for your surgeon.

> The virtues give us
> the freedom to love.

This is all common sense. No one would ever get into an airplane with someone who doesn't have the skills of flying. And no one would ever hop on the operating table with someone who doesn't possess the skills of surgery. Yet, in our age, many people jump into business partnerships, friendships, dating relationships, and even marriages without ever asking the fundamental question of virtue: Does this person have *the virtue*—the skills—necessary to live this relationship well? Does this person have honesty, loyalty, patience, generosity, prudence, self-control, and humility? These are just some of the many virtues we need in order to love others and live out our commitments to them.

Value or Virtue?

When I speak at marriage conferences, I often ask spouses two questions. First: "How many of you value your spouse and want to treat him or her well?" Everyone raises their hands. Second: "How many of you do things to hurt your spouse?" Everyone raises their hands again.

It's very easy to *say* I value my spouse, my children, my friends, and my God. And I may sincerely desire to love them all. But it takes much effort, practice, and grace to acquire the virtues I need to actually *be* a good spouse, parent, friend, and Christian. The virtues are like powers within that help us to love others. Indeed, the virtues give us the freedom to love, and without the virtues, we are simply not capable of loving others the way God intends.

This is an important point to make. When I was a teenager and heard people at church talk about the virtues, I had an *individualistic* view of the virtuous life. I had the mistaken impression that virtues were something good merely for my own soul: for my moral development or my spiritual life. Humility, piety, kindness, prudence, temperance—these and other virtues seemed to be simply good qualities every Catholic was supposed to have in order to be a good Christian. The virtues were like badges that made me a good "boy scout" for God.

However, virtue should be understood *relationally*. The virtues are not important merely for our own lives; they are the habitual dispositions—the skills—we need to love God and the people God has placed in our lives. If I lack virtue in certain areas, that doesn't just harm me; it affects the people closest to me. They will suffer the consequences of my lack of virtue! For example, if I lack in the virtue of generosity, I will do selfish things that hurt my spouse. If I lack prudence and spend too many hours preoccupied with work, my kids will feel the effects of the imprudent way I use my time. If I often get overwhelmed with life and become easily irritated, the people in my life will suffer the effects of my lack of patience and perseverance.

This is the most tragic thing about my deficiency in virtue: to the extent that I lack virtue, to that extent I am not free to love. No matter how much I may desire to be a good son of God, a good husband to my wife, and a good father to my children—without virtue, I will not consistently give the best of myself to the Lord, I will not honor and serve my wife effectively, and I will not raise my children as well as I should. They will all feel the consequences of my lack in virtue.

How to Grow in Virtue

We can grow in virtue in three main ways. First, we can learn more about the virtuous life. Simply *knowing* about the virtues is half the battle. If I don't know what to aim for, then I am almost sure to miss my target in life. But if I gain an understanding of the virtuous life, I at least have a chance to work on the areas where I'm falling short and to grow in the virtues I need the most. We can learn about the virtues in the Bible, the *Catechism of the Catholic Church,* and other good Catholic resources.[13] Reading the lives of the saints is particularly beneficial. The saints help us see the virtues in

---

[13] For example, see: Josef Pieper, *The Four Cardinal Virtues* (Notre Dame, IN: University of Notre Dame Press, 1966); Donald DeMarco, *The Heart of Virtue* (San Francisco: Ignatius Press, 1996); John Cuddeback, *True Friendship* (Denver: Epic, 2003); Steven J. Jensen, *Living the Good Life* (Washington, DC: The Catholic University Press, 2013).

action, embodied in a life story, and they give us concrete examples of how to put virtue into practice. Filling our minds with the lives of the saints can inspire us to live more virtuously, as they did.

Second, practice makes perfect. Growing in virtue doesn't happen by chance. It's not as if someone can wake up one morning and say, "I'm going to be more virtuous today," and expect to become a saint overnight. It takes great intentionality and effort over the course of a lifetime. One common recommendation for growing in virtue is to prayerfully identify an area for growth, and then make a resolution each day to fight against that one weakness, to resist temptation, and most of all to put into practice the particular virtue that counters the vice you're struggling with. So if you notice you tend to talk a lot and like to be at the center of attention, make a resolution to make space for others in conversation and take time to listen. If you struggle with being easily discouraged, make a resolution to say a short prayer of entrustment (such as "Jesus I trust in you") the next time you find yourself disheartened. If you find yourself distracted at Mass, make a resolution to read along with the prayers of the liturgy so your mind stays more focused.

Third, ask for God's grace. No matter how much you study the virtues and no matter how much you try to put them into practice, you will run up against your own human limitations. We are fallen and we simply cannot achieve the virtuous life on our own. We need God's help. But with God's grace, we have Christ's divine life in us. Grace enables us to live the virtues and imitate Christ more than we ever could on our own, for it is Christ's love working through us. That's why we should seek God's grace in prayer and the sacraments, especially by frequenting the Eucharist and Confession. Each time we receive the Sacraments we encounter Jesus himself, who strengthens us in our weaknesses and heals us of our bad habits.

Questions for Reflection/Discussion

1. We saw how we are made for relationships. What are the most important relationships in your life? How well are you fulfilling your responsibilities in those relationships? At home? At work? At church? With your friends?

2. In this chapter we discussed the connection between virtue and living our relationships well. But is this true? Do I really need virtue to love the people in my life? If I care about them and value them, why can't I just love them?

3. There are many virtues, such as justice, humility, patience, purity, courage, prudence, self-control, generosity, honoring others, and gratitude. Which virtue do you think you need to work on the most to strengthen your relationships?

4. Virtue involves three qualities: habitually doing the good *easily* and without a struggle, as if it's second nature; doing the good not every once in a while, but *consistently*; and doing the good *joyfully*, without complaint or frustration. Which of those three qualities do you think is hardest for you? Why?

5. The chapter discussed three ways to grow in virtue: learning about the virtues, intentionally practicing the virtues, and depending on God's grace.

a. What can we do to *learn* about the virtues?

b. What are some ways we can more deliberately try to *practice* virtue?

c. Practically, what do we need to do to draw on God's *grace* more to grow in the virtuous life?

Chapter Five

Getting Freedom Right

Are you free to play the violin?

You might say, "Sure. I can pick up a violin and try to play. No one is going to stop me. It's not against the law. I live in a free country. I can play the violin if I want. It's my free choice." But if you were handed a violin and asked to play a complicated piece by Vivaldi, could you do it? Probably not. Not unless you had taken violin lessons for several years, practiced hard, and acquired the skills of a violinist. Without that ability, you are free to make some screeching noise with the violin strings, but you are not free to play a violin concerto—no matter how much you may desire it.

This question about the violin gets to the heart of two very different views of freedom: the classical understanding of freedom and the way people tend to think about freedom today. And it's absolutely crucial we understand the difference. It can make or break a marriage. It can mean the difference between laying solid foundations for a healthy dating relationship and starting another dead-end romance. It can lead us to succeed or fail as parents. If properly understood, an authentic view of freedom can inspire us to live our relationships well and discover true happiness. But if we get it wrong, it can lead us to much disappointment, frustration, and isolation in life.

A lot is riding on getting freedom right.

True Freedom

In the classical understanding, freedom is the ability to perform actions of high quality: the ability to do certain things with excellence.[14] And this requires certain skills. A professional violinist can perform the Vivaldi violin piece with excellence because she has learned the art of violin playing. My toddler, on the other hand, might be able to grab her older brother's violin bow and bang it on the strings, but she is not free to play Vivaldi no matter how hard she tries. She simply doesn't have the ability.

Similarly, is every person in the US free to converse in Chinese? In the classical sense of freedom, no. Only those who have acquired a degree of fluency in this language are free to converse in it. The person who does not have this skill is not free to speak Chinese, no matter how hard he tries and no matter how much he may desire to do so. True freedom requires a certain skill that gives the person the ability to perform actions with excellence. And the same is true with life as a whole.

---

[14] Servais Pinckaers, *The Sources of Christian Ethics* (Washington, DC: CUA Press, 1995), 355.

Not everyone is free to be a good son or daughter, a good spouse, a good parent, or a good friend. To live these relationships with excellence requires certain skills such as generosity, humility, perseverance, and patience—skills known as the virtues. The virtues give us the freedom to love.

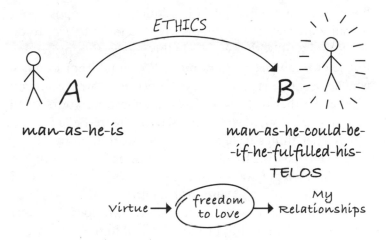

Negative Freedom

Our modern world, however, has a very different notion of freedom. For many, freedom is simply the ability to choose between different options. This kind of liberty can be called "freedom from." In this view, a man possesses freedom when he is free *from* any outside person, group, or law restricting him. *Webster's Dictionary*, for example, reflects this modern view when it defines freedom merely as "the absence of necessity, coercion, or constraint in choice or action."[15] Modern man thinks he has achieved full freedom when he

---

[15] *Merriam-Webster*, s.v. "freedom," http://www.merriam-webster.com/dictionary/freedom.

is free *from* society, institutions, or other people telling him
what to do. Without these outside constraints interfering
with our life choices, we are free to do whatever we want
with our own lives.

This view of freedom leads people to view morality as
something negative or restrictive—an imposition from
the outside that limits one's freedom. "Don't impose your
morality on me!" many people say. "I should be *free* to do
whatever I want with my life." In this perspective, protecting
free choice is what matters most. We should not evaluate
whether a choice is good or bad. It does not matter *what* you
choose. All that matters is *that* you choose for yourself. In
this view, freedom of choice is itself the greatest good.

But other things in life don't really work this way. Sure,
it's good to have the freedom to make choices, but the bigger
question is: What we are going to do with that freedom?
There really are good and bad choices in life. No NBA
basketball player says to his coach, "Hey, it doesn't matter
whether I make the shot or hand the ball to the other team.
All that matters is that I choose." Or imagine a financial
planner saying, "It doesn't matter where you invest your
money. Whether you get a good return or you lose all your
retirement doesn't matter. All that matters is that you are
free to choose."

When it comes to how we live our lives, however, there
is a lot more at stake than a basketball game or a financial
investment. Other people will be affected by our choices. But
the root problem with the modern notion of freedom is that it
puts the self at the center and disregards our responsibilities
to others. Modern man says, "It's my life. Don't tell me what
to do with my life. I am free to do whatever I want with my
life." Notice how self-centered that sounds! Indeed, Pope St.
John Paul II called this modern understanding of liberty "an

individualistic concept of freedom," one which "exalts the isolated individual." [16] Instead of finding freedom in loving the people God has placed in my life, I find freedom when I separate myself from them—from my parents, family, friends, coworkers, community—and decide for myself whatever I want to do with my life. I might choose to care for my parents in their old age, but if I choose not to, that's fine, too. It's my choice. I might choose to give my life to my spouse and kids, but if I choose to leave them for someone else, that's fine, too. It's my life. I might tell my girlfriend I love her because I really do want to marry her. Or I might say it just so I can sleep with her. Either way is okay because I'm free to do whatever I want with my life.

> The modern notion of freedom trains us to become slaves to our selfishness.

This is the tragedy of the modern notion of freedom. When I train myself in the name of my personal freedom to pursue what I want, when I want, how I want, as often as I want, I'm actually not free. I'm a slave. I become a slave to my own interests. It's not easy for me to make sacrifices for others, to serve other people's needs, because I'm always doing what I want and keeping my options open to what is enjoyable for me. In the end, the modern notion of freedom trains us to become slaves to our own selfishness. Only the man who possesses virtue is free to be a good husband, a good father, a good friend. Only the virtuous can consistently perform generous, humble, patient, self-sacrificial acts to serve the

---

[16] John Paul II, *Evangelium Vitae* ("The Gospel of Life"), 19, http://w2.vatican. va/content/john-paul-ii/en/encyclicals/documents/hf_jp-ii_enc_25031995_ evangelium-vitae.html.

people in their lives. The virtuous are free to love because they are not enslaved to their selfish desires.

Sadly, our commitments and responsibilities toward others are often viewed as limitations on our freedom, getting in the way of what we selfishly want to do. Instead of being the arena where I find my happiness in life, my commitments to others are viewed as a ball and chain, weighing me down and keeping me from doing what I want. As Pope Benedict once said, the culture of relativism recognizes nothing as definitive, and thus "leaves as the ultimate criterion only the self with its desires. And under the semblance of freedom it becomes a prison for each one, for it separates people from one another, locking each person into his or her own 'ego.'"[17] This focus on the self separates us from our most fundamental life relationships:

> If the autonomous subject has the last word, then its desires are simply unlimited. It then wants to snatch as much from life as it can get out of it. This, I think really a very major problem of life today. People say: Life is basically complicated and short; I want to get as much out of it as possible, and no one has the right to stand in my way. Before all else I have to be able to seize my piece of it, to fulfill myself, and no one has the right to interfere with me. Anyone who would stand in my way is an enemy of my very self.[18]

It's a Wonderful Life

A model for true freedom can be found in Frank Capra's classic film, *It's a Wonderful Life*. One thing that makes this

---

[17] Pope Benedict XVI, "Address of His Holiness Benedict XVI to the Participants in the Ecclesial Diocesan Convention of Rome," (Basilica of St. John Lateran, June 6, 2005), http://w2.vatican.va/content/benedict-xvi/en/speeches/2005/june/documents/hf_ben-xvi_spe_20050606_convegno-famiglia.html.

[18] Joseph Cardinal Ratzinger, *Salt of the Earth*, ed. Peter Seewald, trans. Adrian Walker (San Francisco: Ignatius Press, 1997), 167.

story so inspiring to generation after generation is that it showcases ordinary, everyday heroism—a heroism everyone can relate to. Unlike most heroes today, the beloved main character, George Bailey, finds his adventure not in sports or on the battlefield in some foreign land. Rather, George discovers his great adventure in the middle of his normal daily life with his family, friends, and community in the small town of Bedford Falls.

George certainly had dreams full of travel, excitement, university studies, and seeing the world, but those plans gave way one by one to a deeper sense of responsibility to his family and community. As his life goes on, he starts to feel frustration and regret as he watches those he grew up with living their dreams while he remains in Bedford Falls. When tragedy strikes and he is in danger of going to prison because of someone else's mistake, he despairs and considers suicide, wondering if his life has meaning and whether all his sacrifices were worth it.

Just at this moment, his guardian angel, Clarence, appears to help him see the profound meaning of his life again. Clarence does this by showing him what Bedford Falls would be like if George had never been born. He takes George on a tour through the town, visiting all the people whom George had impacted throughout the years: his mother, wife, uncle, the local druggist, a girl he knew from childhood. But in this world without George Bailey, his mother ends up a cranky and suspicious old widow, his wife a nervous spinster, his uncle a crazy man, the druggist a ruined drunk, and his childhood friend a prostitute. The town itself is now controlled by the antagonist of the film, the greedy banker and Bailey family rival Mr. Potter, who has the people of Bedford Falls under his thumb, all because George Bailey was never there to stop him. At the end of this journey through a George Bailey-less

Bedford Falls, George realizes the enormous gap left by his absence—and just how wonderful his life really is. And his life is, in fact, wonderful precisely because he chose to live for something much bigger than himself and the pursuit of his own interests. He used his freedom to live for others. In the words of author William Kilpatrick:

> The life of George Bailey is a hero's story. He is, moreover, a hero we can readily identify with. His heroism is the heroism of sustained commitment in the face of unlooked-for burdens and unforeseen turns of fate. His heroism, like that of most adults, consists in *refusing the temptation to be free and uncommitted.*[19]

Being free in the sense of being uncommitted. That's what modern man aims for. Always keeping options open. Not wanting to be tied down. But living this way never satisfies the desires of the heart. It isolates us. It leaves us restless, always hankering for something more. Only when we give up our freedom to do whatever we selfishly want all the time (modern freedom), do we discover a greater freedom: the freedom to love. Only in relationships of sustained commitment will we find our happiness.

The Freedom to Love

True freedom is *not* the popular modern notion of "freedom from"—freedom from people, freedom from responsibility, freedom from others telling me what to do, freedom to do as I please. Rather, true freedom is freedom *for* something: freedom for friendship and freedom for love. It is found in the ability to die to one's self—in giving up one's freedom to do whatever one wants—in order to serve the good of

---

[19] William Kilpatrick, *Why Johnny Can't Tell Right from Wrong* (New York: Touchstone, 1992), 203. Emphasis added.

another person. As Karol Wojtyla (who would become Pope John Paul II) once explained,

> Love consists of a commitment which limits one's freedom—it is a giving of the self, and to give oneself means just that: to limit one's freedom on behalf of another. Limitation of one's freedom might seem to be something negative and unpleasant, but love makes it a positive, joyful and creative thing. *Freedom exists for the sake of love.*[20]

Although many in our modern world see such limitations on their freedom as something confining, we should see it as liberating. After all, I don't want to be a slave to my selfish desires. I want to be free to love my parents, my wife, my children, my friends, and most of all, my God!

This point was driven home to me in marriage. When I was single, I could choose to live where I wanted, work where I wanted, spend my money how I wanted, and spend my time how I wanted. I was "free" in the modern sense—free to do what I wanted. But when I got married and started having children, my life changed dramatically. I couldn't just do what *I* wanted all the time. I couldn't come home and say, "Hi honey. I spent all our money on the way home from work tonight and bought a new sports car." Or, "I quit my job today and I'm moving to California . . . want to come with me?" or, "Hey, I'm going to hang out with my friends this weekend. Hope you have fun with the kids." As a husband and father, I need to think constantly about what is best for my family, not just what I want to do in life.

> "Freedom exists for the sake of love."
> —Pope St. John Paul II

I could view my wife and children only as limitations on my freedom, people who are constantly restricting me and

---

[20] Karol Wojtyla, *Love and Responsibility* (New York: Farrar, Straus & Giroux, 1981), 135.

preventing me from doing what I want all the time. But these limitations are good for me. They help me get outside myself and live for something bigger. And my life is so much enriched by them. Sure, I could have more money, more free time, more sleep, and more energy if I didn't have to care for these people in my life. But would I be happier? No way. I wouldn't trade anything in the world for Beth, Madeleine, Paul, Teresa, Karl, Luke, Josephine, Chiara, and Elinor. They have enriched my life in so many ways, expanding my heart and helping me grow in love.

And that's the great mystery of love. In other transactions in life, if I give something away, then I don't have it anymore. If I give you a twenty-dollar bill, I have twenty dollars less in my wallet. But love is different. When I give of myself in love to another person, I don't lose anything. Rather, I gain something more. My life is profoundly enriched. I find a greater joy and happiness in life because I'm living the way God has made me: for self-giving love.

Questions for Reflection/Discussion

1. Let's review: In your own words, what is the difference between the modern notion of freedom and the classical view of freedom?

2. The modern tendency is to want to be free and uncommitted. Not to be tied down. What are some ways you see this in our culture? What are some ways you notice this in your own life?

3. Put yourself in the shoes of George Bailey in *It's a Wonderful Life*. How would you have felt about all your friends pursuing their dreams while you stayed

back at home to care for the family business and the needs of the town? How do you think most young people today would think about the prospects of being George Bailey?

4. Karol Wojtyla said, "Love consists of a commitment which limits one's freedom—it is a giving of the self, and to give oneself means just that: to limit one's freedom on behalf of another." In what ways do you think love consists of a limiting of one's freedom? Have you experienced this?

5. Jesus describes the mystery of self-giving love when he says, "Whoever loses his life for my sake will find it" (Mt 16:25). In what ways have you experienced this mystery of your life being enriched by making sacrifices for someone?

6. In your life right now, identify some areas where you can grow in this kind of self-giving love.

Chapter Six

Law and Happiness

The very idea of a moral law is like a bad word today. "Moral law" sounds like a bunch of random rules and restrictions—one group telling others how to live their lives. The mere mention that certain things are right and wrong for everyone immediately makes people uncomfortable or frustrated, even angry. Picture yourself trying to convince a friend a certain action is morally wrong for everyone all the time. Here are the kind of thoughts that might be going through your friend's mind:

- "Really? How could this possibly be an issue?"
- "You're only saying this because you're a Christian."
- "Only people who can't think for themselves blindly follow what their church says."
- "You've been brainwashed."
- "This is just the way you've been raised."
- "You must be very insecure—I guess morality helps you feel okay with yourself."
- "Your morality makes you feel superior, like you're better than other people."

- "What is right and wrong can and should change as the times change. We shouldn't be so rigid and out of touch."
- "Who are you to make your particular way of looking at the world a moral law for everyone?"

Talking about a moral law sparks strong reactions today. But part of the challenge is that many people don't understand the "why" behind the moral law. When asked why Christians think God gives moral laws like the Ten Commandments or the Sermon on the Mount, many people would say something like, "So they can be good and get to Heaven." It is generally assumed that Christian moral laws about marriage, sexuality, care for those in need, and protecting human life are simply rules believers have to follow or are some test of obedience so that they can please their Almighty God. But the actual Christian view of the moral law is so much bigger than this.

More Than a Test

What would you think if I gave my toddler the following test: I sit him down on the living room floor and surround him with his favorite toys and treats—piles of blocks, trains, cars, and boats, with dozens of lollipops, cookies, and bowls of ice cream all around. Picture his huge smile, his eyes glowing with excitement. He has entered toddler heaven! He looks at me, as if to ask, "Is this really true? Is this all for me?" Then he looks at the ice cream and starts to reach for it. Just at that moment, however, I sternly look him in the eye and shout, "No! Don't touch anything!"

"Why Dada?" he asks.

"Don't ask why! Just do as I say or you will be punished. I'm testing whether you will be obedient to me!"

No loving father would do this. Yet, sadly, this is how many Christians understand God's moral law: a random rule we have to follow, a test of obedience, or something that makes us a "good person" so we can get to Heaven. If this is how Christians view morality—as random hoops we have to jump through to please our Heavenly Father—then it's no wonder so many people in our world today doubt that a moral law really exists. It all seems rather arbitrary, and in the end, irrelevant for my daily life here on earth.

But what if I were to tell you that the moral law is all about love—God's love for us and a way for us to grow in love? What if I were to tell you that the moral law is not an arbitrary rule, but corresponds to the deepest desires of our hearts? What if I were to tell you that the moral law is all about happiness and finding fulfillment in life? In this chapter, we will see that the moral law is an expression of God's love for us. He made us, he knows how we work, and he gave us the moral law so we would live well and be happy.

A Light for My Path

Morality is the quest for happiness. The pre-Christian philosopher Aristotle, for example, understood this. His entire treatment on ethics is basically an answer to the fundamental question, "How do we find happiness?" The ancient Jewish people also saw morality not as a bunch of random rules, but as something helpful for living a happy life: a lamp to our feet and a light to our path (cf. Ps 119:105). Similarly, when Jesus gave the Sermon on the Mount, he began not with rules but with the eight famous blessings known as the Beatitudes—a vision for how to live a blessed, happy life (cf. Mt 5:3–12). And when the Catholic theologian St. Thomas Aquinas began his treatment on morality, he focuses on the question: In what does happiness consist? [21]

This is the Christian view of morality: God gives the moral law because he loves us and wants us to be happy. A good father, for example, might give laws to his children for their well-being—because he loves them and wants what is best for them. He wants his children to be happy. The law is an expression of the father's love. This point was driven home to me years ago, when my then thirteen-month old son tried to climb the monkey bars in our backyard. I quickly realized we needed to issue a new "law" for him.

> My thirteen-month old son reached out for the monkey bars and suddenly found himself stuck, hanging for dear life seven feet in the air.

I was inside the house when it happened. After observing his older siblings repeatedly climb a ladder and race across the monkey bars on our backyard play set, little Karl decided he wanted to give it a try. He set out on his adventure when no one was looking and made it all the way up the ladder. From there, he reached out for the first rung of the monkey bars with both hands and suddenly found himself stuck, hanging for dear life seven feet in the air.

His older siblings noticed him and immediately rushed inside screaming, "Karl's stuck on the monkey bars! Karl's stuck on the monkey bars!" I dashed outside and found him dangling with arms completely outstretched, both hands clinging desperately to the wooden bar and a look of horror

---

[21] St. Thomas Aquinas, *Summa Theologica*, I-II, 2,1. For more, see "Of Those Things in Which Man's Happiness Consists (Eight Articles)", http://www.sacred-texts.com/chr/aquinas/summa/sum135.htm.

on his face. His older brother was below him, propping him up until I came. The boy was rescued, but I knew I needed to declare a new "law" that day: little Karl was not allowed to climb the monkey bars! I issued this monkey-bar decree not because I was on a power trip with my thirteen-month old. Rather, I gave this law because I love him and wanted to protect him from getting hurt. And the same is true with God's moral law. He made us. He knows how we work. And he gave us the moral law to guide us on the pathway to what will bring us true happiness in life.

The Instruction Manual

God's moral law is like an instruction manual for our lives. When we purchase a car, we receive an owner's manual that tells how best to operate the vehicle. The manufacturer knows how the car works and instructs us about what we need to do to operate the car properly. No one views these instructions as impositions on our lives to restrict our freedom. They are given to help us use the vehicle well.

A friend of mine once purchased a Fisher Price exersaucer for her baby—one of those play saucers with a bouncy seat in the middle and lots of gadgets around it for the baby to play with. She told me that the instruction manual for the saucer had some interesting warnings such as, "This play saucer does not float ... Do not use in water" (Imagine a parent taking little Johnny waterskiing on the play saucer!) and my favorite: "Do not use for sledding" (Imagine six-month old Johnny zooming down the snowy hill in the play saucer!).

Now what would you think if I purchased an exersaucer, read the instruction manual, and tore it up, angrily saying, "Fisher Price, who are you to tell me what to do with my exersaucer? This is *my* exersaucer. And I have the right to do whatever

I want with *my* exersaucer. Don't impose your views about exersaucers on me!" Am I free to take my kids waterskiing or sledding on my exersaucer? Sure. But I'll probably ruin my baby's life in the process. Similarly, can we use our free will to go against God's moral law? Yes. But when we do so, we will do harm to ourselves and to others. When we break God's moral law, we break ourselves in the end.

You see, the moral law is like God's instruction manual for our lives. God is the "divine manufacturer." He made us and knows how we work. He knows that certain actions will lead us to our happiness while other acts will lead us to frustration and emptiness for ourselves and others. As Pope St. John Paul II once explained: "God, who alone is good, knows perfectly what is good for man, and by virtue of his very love proposes this good to man in the commandments." [22] The moral law is thus the pathway to our *telos*, to our happiness.

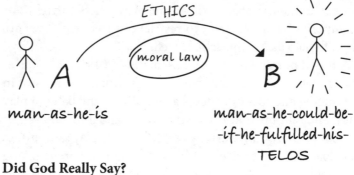

Did God Really Say?

But if the law is for our happiness, why are there such harsh reactions to the very idea of a moral truth today? One famous

[22] John Paul II, *Veritatis Splendor* ("The Splendor of Truth"), 35, http://w2.vatican.va/content/john-paul-ii/en/encyclicals/documents/hf_jp-ii_enc_06081993_veritatis-splendor.html.

story from the Judeo-Christian tradition can help shed light on this. It's a story you've probably heard before, many of you since your childhood. But I invite you now as an adult to take a closer look at this marvelous account. It's a story filled with much symbolism, subtlety, and literary art, and one that gives us a glimpse into what really happened in the origins of the human family: the story of Adam and Eve in the Garden of Eden.

First, consider carefully what the Bible says about the one prohibition God gives to Adam and Eve after putting them in the garden: "You may freely eat of every tree of the garden; but of the tree of the knowledge of good and evil you shall not eat, for in the day that you eat of it you shall die" (Gn 2:16–17). Notice how God does not give this law to Adam in order to control him or test his obedience. In fact, God's words underscore the broad liberty he was giving Adam: he may eat *freely* from *every* other tree in the garden. There is only one tree from which God does not want Adam to eat. Why is this? God warns Adam about this one tree, the tree of knowledge of good and evil, because he does not want Adam to be harmed: "*For in the day that you eat of it you shall*

> "Fisher Price, who are you to tell me what to do with my exersaucer? This is *my* exersaucer. Don't impose your views about exersaucers on me!"

die." In other words, God gives this law to protect Adam from some mysterious danger represented by the tree of knowledge of good and evil (see CCC 396).[23]

---

[23] "The 'tree of knowledge of good and evil' symbolically evokes the insurmountable limits that man, being a creature, must freely recognize and respect with trust. Man is dependent on his Creator and subject to the laws of creation and to the moral norms that govern the use of freedom" (CCC 396).

Rules vs. Relationship

The law, then, flows from God's love, and he gives this law to protect Adam and Eve. But the devil wants Adam and Eve (and all of us) to view God's law *apart* from his love—to see the command merely as a rule, not as an expression of God's relationship with us.

Now consider the serpent's first words to Eve: "Did God say, 'You shall not eat of any trees of the garden?'" (Gn 3:1). First, the serpent simply refers to the Lord as "God" (*Elohim* in Hebrew). This title is used in Genesis 1 to describe God as the Creator of the universe. The serpent's use of this title here is particularly striking because the rest of Genesis 2–3 characteristically refers to God as the "Lord God" (*Yahweh Elohim* in Hebrew), which elsewhere in the Bible expresses God's intimacy with his people as Israel's covenant partner. In Genesis 2, it is the "Lord God" who creates man from the ground and breathes life into him, who creates the animals and allows Adam to name them, and who creates the woman from Adam's side. Indeed, the "Lord God" is a loving God who is involved in Adam and Eve's lives, providing for them as his children.

> The devil is not simply trying to get Adam and Eve to break a rule. Ultimately, he is trying to get them to break a relationship.

But the serpent will have none of this. He wants Eve to think of God as a remote deity who burdens them with this law. It is as if the serpent is saying, "Did that distant Creator say, 'You shall not eat of *any* trees of the garden'?" The serpent wants them to think of God as an oppressive lawmaker whose arbitrary rule limits their freedom.

The woman responds to the serpent by mentioning that they can eat from other trees and that if they eat from the tree in the midst of the garden they would die (see Gn 3:2–3). To this, the serpent replies: "You will not die. For God knows that when you eat of it your eyes will be opened, and you will be like God, knowing good and evil" (Gn 3:4).

Attack on God's Fatherhood

Feel the gravity of the serpent's words. In saying, "You will *not* die," the serpent is basically calling God a liar. According to the serpent, the tree is *not* harmful, but actually something that will make them like God—and God is so afraid of Adam and Eve eating from the tree and becoming like him that he makes up this law to keep them under his control.

Notice how the devil is not simply trying to get Adam and Eve to break a rule. Ultimately, he is trying to get them to break a relationship. At its root, the first sin involves Adam and Eve questioning God's goodness. As the *Catechism* explains, "Man, tempted by the devil, *let his trust in his Creator die in his heart* and, abusing his freedom, disobeyed God's command. This is what man's first sin consisted of. All subsequent sin would be disobedience toward God and *lack of trust in his goodness*" (CCC 397, emphasis added).

The fall of Adam and Eve is the story of all humanity, but especially of our modern age. As he did with our first parents, the devil causes us to doubt that there is a God who loves us so much that he reveals a moral law for our benefit. Deep in the hearts of many modern men and women is sown the serpent's doubt: "Did God really say ... ?" [24]

This is the tragedy of moral relativism. It causes us to see the moral law as an obstacle standing in the way of what we want

---

[24] How we can come to know with confidence *what* God has really revealed is a topic addressed in the postscript.

to do, instead of something that helps us discover authentic happiness. In a relativistic culture, we doubt that God's law is really a trustworthy pathway to happiness and wisdom for navigating through the challenges of life. Like Adam and Eve, we think we know a better way. But we cannot divorce God's law from his love. Thus, when we reject God's moral law for our own preferences, we are ultimately rejecting the Father's loving care for us.

Questions for Reflection/Discussion

1. Why does God give a moral law? How would you explain this to your friends?

2. In what ways is God's moral law more about *relationship* than *rules*?

3. In Genesis 2:16–17, God told Adam, "You may freely eat of every tree of the garden; but of the tree of the knowledge of good and evil you shall not eat, for in the day that you eat of it you shall die." According to these verses, why did God tell Adam not to eat from this tree?

4. In Genesis 3:4, the serpent tells Eve nothing bad will happen if she eats from that tree: "You will not die. For God knows that when you eat of it your eyes will be opened, and you will be like God." What is the serpent ultimately saying about God? In other words, how does he want Adam and Eve to view God and God's law?

5. How do we see men and women buying into the serpent's lies about the moral law today?

6. The *Catechism* teaches, "Man, tempted by the devil, let his trust in his Creator die in his heart" and that all subsequent sin is ultimately a "lack of trust in his goodness" (CCC 937). How might sin be a lack of trust in God's goodness? What are some ways you lack trust in your heart when you are tempted to sin? What are some ways we can overcome that lack of trust?

Chapter Seven

The Art of Living

I never imagined taking my son to piano lessons would be so fascinating. At each early morning lesson, I found myself learning so much—not just about the piano, but about life itself.

At first, the experience was painful. The teacher demanded a lot of her students: one hour of practice each day and mastery of each piece before moving on to the next song. Could my six-year-old boy handle this? With his previous piano instructor, he had whizzed through several new pieces every couple of weeks. He seemed quite successful, but now it looked like he was going backwards. Each lesson was packed with corrections and instructions on how to improve.

The teacher focused on small details: posture, hand position, relaxed arm muscles, curved fingers, and how to touch each key. She emphasized proper fingering, rhythm, dynamics, and just the right balance between the left and right hand. Crescendos and diminuendos, soft *piano* notes and loud *forte* notes, accents, ornaments, and trills all had to be mastered.

She also shared stories of the great classical composers—lessons from their lives, their work ethic, their technique, and the innovations they brought to the world of music.

Over time, I began to see that he was undergoing a beautiful apprenticeship. He was learning from a master who was passionate about her craft and was immersing her students in the long tradition of piano playing that she had come to love. She herself had undertaken a thorough training from her childhood all the way up to graduate studies in which she learned from the masters of her day and became an accomplished pianist in her own right. Now in her late seventies, she was carefully passing on to a new generation of pianists the basic knowledge, skills, and techniques necessary not simply to play the piano, but to do so with excellence.

Soon, words such as *crescendo, staccato,* and *andante* were becoming part of my son's regular vocabulary. Through his teacher's stories, Bach, Mozart, and Beethoven were, in a sense, becoming some of his mentors. And after mastering a number of the basic skills in his early months of piano boot camp, he quickly started moving along from "*Happy Birthday*" and "*Silent Night*" to Haydn's *Piano Concerto in C.*

The Craft of Life

In order to master a craft, we need to undergo a kind of apprenticeship. We need to be mentored by those who have been formed in a certain tradition and who have mastered the skills associated with it. The same is true with life. Life is like a craft. To live it well requires knowing what the good life is, and acquiring the skills, or virtues, needed to live in that way. As we discussed earlier, a human life is fundamentally about relationships—our relationship with God and with those he has placed in our lives. A good life, therefore, is one in which someone fulfills his relationships. And one needs the virtues—patience, humility, self-control, generosity—to live relationships well.

Thankfully, there is a long tradition on the virtues and how to raise children, how to build a good marriage, how to be a good friend, and how to grow in a relationship with God. We can learn from those who have gone before us and from those presently among us who have mastered the art of living life with excellence. From a Catholic perspective, this tradition is found in the wisdom of the Bible, the Church's teachings, the Liturgy, and the saints. Through the centuries it has found expression culturally in literature, music, art, and poems inspired by the Catholic Faith, as well as many books and manuals on the virtues, the spiritual life, and human relationships. But most of all, this tradition, this "art of living" as Pope Benedict has called it, is passed on from person-to-person, heart-to-heart, within a Christian community of men and women who embody the virtues and impart the good life to the next generation.

Unfortunately, modernity has taught young people to view the Christian tradition with suspicion—to see it not as an aid to living a happy life, but as an oppressive, restrictive force that prevents us from discovering for ourselves the meaning of our existence and charting our own course in life.

This suspicion of tradition is deeply rooted in modern philosophy. The eighteenth-century German philosopher Immanuel Kant famously challenged European intellectuals to question the traditions they had received and to become "independent thinkers" who are "free from outside direction." No longer was the Christian path seen as a helpful apprenticeship in which one learns the art of living from the Christian tradition and a virtuous community. For Kant, willingness to submit to such an apprenticeship or tutelage was infantile. He instead called men and women to grow up and achieve enlightenment, which for Kant meant "man's release from his self-incurred tutelage." Kant celebrated the enlightened man for "throwing off the yoke of tutelage" and "thinking for himself." [25]

A Culture of Independent Thinkers

But what happens when the Christian tradition is viewed as an oppressive yoke, as Kant describes? This outlook on life cuts us off from the very resource that helps us flourish. A wise piano student would not view the tradition of musical notation, chords, tone, and technique as oppressive. And he would not refuse the mentoring of a good teacher, saying "I don't want anyone's help! I'm an independent thinker! I want to learn it all by myself!"

Yet imagine that you are a young child who wants to learn how to play the piano and are told to go figure it out on your own. No one mentions that there are piano teachers who could help you. No one gives you any books. No one teaches you how to read music. You are simply told to be your own piano player and play however you want. There's no *right* way to play the piano.

Now imagine that after years of pecking at the keyboard, you, at the age of twenty-two, discover others who play the piano a lot better than you. You are inspired by them and have a burning desire to play like them. They perform beautiful pieces by Chopin, Beethoven, and Haydn—composers unfamiliar to you. You hear your new friends talking about

25 Immanuel Kant, "What is Enlightenment?" in Immanuel Kant, *On History*, ed. Lewis White Beck, trans. Lewis White Beck, Robert E. Anchor, and Emil L. Facken-heim (Indianapolis: Bobbs-Merrill, 1963), 3-10.

major and minor scales, chords, and cadences—words that sound like a foreign language to you. Moreover, you find many books about how to play the piano that could have been very helpful. On top of all that, you discover that many teachers would have happily formed you into an excellent pianist.

Perhaps this grand tradition of music was kept from you because your community, your government, your teachers at school, your heroes in Hollywood, and maybe even your own parents or church mistakenly viewed it as something irrelevant and out-of-date, or even worse, as something harmful to your development as a pianist. Whatever the case may be, you now realize that you have been cheated. Yes, cheated! There has been this beautiful tradition of music that would have been very helpful, but it was withheld from you and all because some people didn't want

> Whatever the case may be, you now realize that you have been cheated. Yes, cheated!

to impose it on you? You come to see that the independent approach to learning the piano has left you with kindergarten level skill and that your self-taught rendition of *Three Blind Mice* does not hold a candle to what these trained pianists have achieved. You sadly realize that because this formation was withheld, you are unable to play the piano with excellence.

Why Didn't Anyone Tell Me?

Similarly, there is a great tradition of the virtues and the good life that is no longer being passed on from generation to generation. Many parents, teachers, and leaders do not even know such wisdom for life exists. And others who do know of it deliberately hold it back because they view it as something negative, restrictive, or harmful. Thus, while many young people are trained to become good doctors, businessmen, and engineers, they do not receive an apprenticeship in what matters most—the art of living. They might be prepared to build successful careers, but will they be successful in their marriages? In raising children? In authentic friendship? In their relationship with God?

When it comes to a vision for life, the only clear guidance young people get from our relativistic culture is, "Do whatever you want. Be whoever you want to be. It doesn't matter how you live your life, as long as you are happy." With such meaningless advice, it's no wonder many college students today find themselves anxiously trying to figure out what it means to be a man or a woman, how to date, and how to interact with the opposite sex. Many young couples enter marriage not knowing the basics of how to build a good marriage and very unsure about how to raise children, discipline them, and form their characters. We learn the Periodic Table of Elements and multiplication tables in school but have not been taught the art of living.

> Many young people might be prepared to build successful careers, but will they be successful in their marriages? In raising children? In their relationship with God?

When people later in life discover the rich wisdom of the tradition of the virtues, they often feel cheated by their upbringing, their education, and the culture. When college students and young adults learn the Church's teachings on love, relationships, and sexuality, they often cry out, "Why didn't anyone teach me this earlier in life? It would have saved me from so much pain and heartache!" When married couples come across the Christian vision for love and marriage, they say, "We wish we had learned this a lot earlier in our marriage!" Parents regretting choices they made in raising their children lament, "I would have done things so differently with my children if only I had known all this earlier in my life."

If you feel this way, don't despair. God's grace can overcome deficiencies in our formation. Indeed, there have been numerous saints who got started in life on the wrong path but later were changed through God's truth and mercy. Still, if we want to give others and ourselves the best chance to thrive in life, it is crucial that society recovers and imparts once again the tradition of the virtues. If the art of living is passed on, more people will be prepared to succeed in life—and fewer will have to say, "Why didn't anyone tell me this before?"

Questions for Reflection/Discussion

1. What do you appreciate most about your upbringing—the ways your parents, schools, church, and society have prepared you for life? In what areas do you wish you received more training for life—for friendship, dating, living a virtuous life, marriage, parenting, living as a child of God?

2. In what ways might the modern mistrust of tradition hinder us from learning the art of living life well?

3. Some people say they have been cheated out of a formation in what matters most: living our relationships with excellence. Have you experienced that to some extent? Why or why not?

4. Practically, what's something you can do right now to gain more formation in the virtues and the art of living?

5. What are some ways God can help make up for what we might have lacked in our formation so far?

PART THREE

SEVEN KEYS FOR RESPONDING
TO RELATIVISM

SEVEN KEYS FOR RESPONDING TO RELATIVISM

It's time now to get practical. We've laid the foundations of a classical moral worldview and walked through the connections between virtue, grace, freedom, friendship, the moral law, and the art of living. Understanding each of these aspects and the inner coherence of this view is powerful for evangelization. It helps you pinpoint some of the root problems of the relativistic outlook. And it helps you move beyond the superficial and oftentimes emotionally-charged discussions people have about morality today. Most of all, it gives you a framework for addressing particular questions that will inevitably come up for which you could never fully prepare in advance.

Still, we need some specific action points: "What should I do? What do I say?" Part Three of this book offers seven keys to responding to our relativistic friends. As we've seen, there is no quick fix to the problem of moral relativism. So these seven keys should not be taken as proofs or apologetic arguments for disproving relativism in thirty seconds or less. These are more like general principles and tips to guide you as you accompany a friend in a longer term relationship. Think of these seven points as tools for you to have on hand—keys in your pocket—to use in your conversations when appropriate. They relate to crucial attitudes and approaches that will help you open the door to moral truth in their lives.

The seven keys are:

1. Lead with Mercy

2. "Relativism Wounds People"

3. Law = Love

4. Making Judgments vs. Judging Souls

5. Relativism Is Not Neutral

6. Relativism Is a Mask

7. Taking on the Heart of Christ

Key One

Lead with Mercy

One of Pope Francis's favorite images for the Church in the modern world is that of a field hospital. Like the medical care offered to the seriously injured on a battle field, the Church urgently needs to go out to the many people who have been wounded by the secular, relativistic culture in which we live.

We saw the problem in the previous chapter: As the world turns away from the Gospel and traditional values, we haven't just lost the Christian Faith. We've lost the art of living. We don't know how to have a good marriage, how to parent well, how to have strong friendships and dating relationships, or how to care for the poor and suffering around us. As a result, people get hurt. "Humanity is wounded, deeply wounded," Pope Francis has said. "Relativism wounds people."[26] With no moral compass guiding our lives, many have been injured by the culture, by people around them, and by their own misguided choices.

This is why we need to go out to the world armed not just with the moral law, but also with mercy, as Pope Francis describes: "I believe this is a time for mercy. The Church is

---

[26] Pope Francis, *The Name of God is Mercy*, ed. Andrea Tornielli, trans. Oonagh Stransky (New York: Random House, 2016), 15.

showing her maternal side, her motherly face, to a humanity
that is wounded. She does not wait for the wounded to knock
on her doors, she looks for them on the streets, she gathers
them in, she embraces them, she takes care of them, she
makes them feel loved."[27] To cure the wound of relativism,
we need to *lead with mercy.*

Getting to the Heart of the Gospel

When helping the seriously wounded on a battlefield, the
doctor in the field hospital doesn't offer wellness checkups. If
a soldier has been shot in the chest or has a ruptured spleen,
the doctor doesn't begin by asking, "How is your cholesterol
level?" The most serious wounds need to be addressed first.

Similarly, when talking with your relativistic friends
about a moral issue, be aware that they might have more
serious wounds other than their misunderstanding about
the particular topic you're debating. They might not know
how much God loves them, has a plan for them, and wants
them to be happy. They
might not know how God
longs to bestow his mercy
on them, forgive them, and
offer them a fresh start in
life. They might not know
how much God wants to heal
them of whatever burdens they may be carrying, whether
it is wounds from their past (a parent not involved in their
lives, growing up in a broken home, abuse, feeling not good
enough, disappointing others, feeling unworthy of love)
or wounds from their present (breakups, feeling used in

> If a soldier has been shot in
> the chest, the doctor doesn't
> begin by asking, "How is
> your cholesterol level?"

---

[27] Ibid., 6.

relationships, bad habits, pressure to achieve, isolation, an unhappy marriage, a divorce, feeling a failure as a parent).

People need to know the heart of the Gospel, not just a list of moral condemnations. They need to know these basic truths: God is madly in love with you. The God who is love, created you out of love, and has a plan for your life. He invites you to share in his love and, even though you turned away from him, he constantly seeks you, out of love, to restore you to himself. He is so in love with you he sent his Son, Jesus Christ, to die for you so that you can be reunited with him. He wants to forgive you, and to heal you of whatever wounds and burdens you carry. He wants a personal relationship with you and wants you to follow him so you can be happy in this life and be with him forever in Heaven.

This is the heart of the Gospel—the story of Christ's saving love. The heart of the Gospel is not simply "gay marriage and abortion are morally wrong" or "contraception separates the unitive and procreative aspects of marriage." Let me be clear: the Church's teachings on human life, sexuality, and marriage are essential. We all need to know them and follow them. These important moral teachings flow from the Gospel message. But when it comes to evangelization, Pope St. John Paul II, Pope Benedict XVI, and Pope Francis recommend initial proclamation of the Gospel come first. Then, after that important foundation, more in-depth catechesis and drawing out the moral consequences of the Gospel follows.[28]

To use an analogy, imagine a child who has strong allergic reactions to dogs. If that child played with a shaggy dog one day and had a severe asthmatic attack, would your first interaction with the child be, "Don't you know you shouldn't

---

[28] For more on this, see Edward Sri, *Pope Francis and the Joy of the Gospel: Rediscovering the Heart of a Disciple.* (Huntington, IN; Our Sunday Visitor, 2014).

be touching dogs? Let me give you seven reasons why you should not be playing with dogs. ... " Of course not. You'd have to address the most pressing need first: You would be focused on getting the kid breathing again! Then later, after he has recovered, you might give him the lecture on avoiding contact with dogs.

Truth and Mercy

Many people today are so wounded by the relativistic culture that they do not know the basics—the basics of how to live life well and the basics of the Gospel message. If we focus exclusively on the moral law apart from the story of God's saving love—God's plan for our lives, Christ's saving Death and Resurrection, forgiveness, mercy, grace, the Sacraments—we risk driving people away in two ways.

First, without the wider context of God's saving love and mercy (and especially given the current crisis of reason), people in the secular world simply can't understand why a married couple shouldn't use contraception or why premarital sex is wrong. It just doesn't make sense to them. When these teachings are taken out of the context of God's plan of salvation and our life in Christ, they seem like arbitrary rules from the distant past being imposed on people today. What is supposed to be a light to our feet and a path to human fulfillment comes off as puritanical nonsense and legalistic moralism.

But that's not all. When we single out the moral issues apart from God's tireless mercy and the healing power of his grace, we risk leaving people with discouragement and despair. Without the sacramental life of grace, the Church's beautiful moral teachings seem impossible to follow. People outside the Church can't be expected to turn their lives around magically and practice heroic virtue overnight. They need more than a list of moral condemnations to help them on the way. They need encouragement. They need to know God's patience and mercy with their faults. And they need to know how much God's grace can help them do what they can never do by their own strength.

Take, for example, the problem of pornography, which affects so many people today. Imagine if I were to give a talk to college students about pornography and focused just on the moral law: "Come on. You know this is wrong. This is a serious sin. You are breaking God's law when you do this. Muster up some self-control and quit looking at those dirty images." How helpful would that be? Many people already feel so ashamed and helpless about their addiction. They feel trapped, discouraged, and unable to break free. They need more than just the message of God's law. They need to know the power of God's mercy.

But what if I said something like this instead: "God knows what you're struggling with—and he loves you. He forgives you every time you stumble, as long as you come back to him with repentant hearts. And most of all, he wants to help you. He wants to heal you. No matter how many times you fall, know he's waiting for you to turn back to him, especially in the Sacrament of Reconciliation. Also know that others have been right where you're at in this struggle, and God has changed them. He has liberated them. He has healed them. And he can do the same with you. His grace is powerful." This latter approach, obviously, would be much more effective. Leading with mercy gives people the encouragement they need to follow God's law.

"Neither Do I Condemn You"

What is the sin you're most ashamed of? Maybe it's something you did a long time ago or something you're doing right now. Maybe it's the way you treated someone, the resentment you have toward some relative, or the envy you have of a friend. Perhaps it's the way you spend your money, what you watch on TV, or something in your sexual life. Maybe it's the way you treat your spouse, your kids, your parents, or your peers. Whatever it may be, imagine if that embarrassing sin of yours suddenly came out in the open and everyone knew about it. *How would you feel?* Various emotions could be at work: Shame. Fear. Sorrow. Anger. Fear over what others will think of you or what will happen next. Sorrow that you hurt someone or let someone down. Anger with yourself and with those who exposed you. Regret: wishing you never had done this. Despair: your life will never be the same.

These are some of the emotions the woman in John's Gospel probably felt when her hidden sin of adultery came to light (Jn 8:1–8). Thrown before the Jewish leaders and Jesus, she was accused of adultery and threatened to be stoned to death. She probably felt very alone and afraid at that moment: afraid over what would happen next; angry with her accusers; ashamed, frustrated with herself, and most likely regretting what she had done—wishing she could take it all back. Before anyone else gathered stones to throw at her, she was probably already, in a sense, picking up stones to throw at herself.

Now consider what happens next. Just at this moment of despair and self-condemnation, Jesus looks at her with love and says the most unexpected thing: "Neither do I condemn you; go, and do not sin again" (Jn 8:11).

What an amazing moment that would have been! The woman's whole world was turned around in an instant. Instead of condemnation and punishment, Jesus offers her love, forgiveness, and a second chance. That's the same hope we want to offer people today: a way out, a new start, hope that change is possible, confident they can be forgiven, knowledge that they are loved.

A Second Chance

This woman's story is our story. Maybe we haven't committed adultery, but we all have baggage of various sorts. We have all done things in our lives that we deeply regret and wish we could take back. Many people, however, go through life never facing the truth about their decisions, and carry an uneasy, subtle burden of regret and guilt on their hearts. But just like he did with the woman caught in adultery, Jesus wants to free us from that. He wants to forgive us. He wants to give us a new start in life. He says the same words to us: "Neither do I condemn you; go, and do not sin again."

But if that's the case, why don't more people simply turn to God for help? The twelfth-century mystic St. Bernard of Clairvaux once said that it is because they do not know God to be a God of mercy. In his commentary on the Song of Songs, he writes, "I am certain that they refuse because they imagine this kindly disposed God to be harsh and severe, this merciful God to be callous and inflexible, this lovable God to be cruel and oppressive."[29] And this makes complete sense. If people don't know God's patience, his forgiveness, and his amazing power to heal our weaknesses,

---

[29] St. Bernard of Clairvaux, *On the Song of Songs II*, 38:2, trans. Kilian Walsh (Kalamazoo, MI, Cistercian Publications, 1976).

then why would anyone bother turning back to God? ("I'm trapped. I can't change. There's no way I could live like those Christians.") Without God's help, there's no point in trying. As soon as a man would consider striving for a better life, St. Bernard says, he'd face his own inadequacy and give up in discouragement.

> If he does not know how good God is, how kind and gentle, how willing to pardon, will not his sensually-inspired reason argue with him and say: 'What are you doing? ... Your sins are too grave and too many; nothing that you do, even to stripping the skin from your flesh, can make satisfaction for them ... a lifetime's habits are not easily conquered.' Dismayed by these and similar arguments, the unhappy man quits the struggle, not knowing how easily God's omnipotent goodness could overthrow all these obstacles.[30]

That's why the first thing we have to keep in mind when talking with our relativistic friends is to *lead with mercy*. Behind the moral issue you might be discussing with your friend is a real person who needs God's love and mercy. Don't underestimate the heavy burdens of unhappiness, fear, shame, and guilt many people carry deep in their hearts. Even if they display an air of confidence, self-sufficiency, or disregard for religion, some of the most outwardly successful and self-assured people are aching on the inside. Deep down, many are unsatisfied and longing for something more in life. No matter how much success, money, fame, alcohol, or sex they have, their hearts are still restless. Only God can fill that void.

Two Pillars of Mercy

So as we go out to the world not just with the moral law, but also with the good news of mercy, let's keep in mind the two pillars of mercy: forgiveness and healing.

---

[30] Ibid., 38.1.

The first aspect of God's mercy is forgiveness. We must always communicate how much Jesus longs to forgive us no matter what we've done. He wants to remove whatever barriers keep us from him. All throughout his public ministry, Jesus is driven by a pressing desire to reach out to sinners, tax collectors, prostitutes, Gentiles, and all those who have been separated from God. And he's constantly reaching out to us today, inviting us to turn back to him. He wants us to know that

> "We are not the sum of our weaknesses and failures; we are the sum of our Father's love for us."
> —Pope St. John Paul II

no matter what we've done, our sins do not entirely define us. As Pope St. John Paul once said, *"We are not the sum of our weaknesses and failures; we are the sum of the Father's love for us and our real capacity to become the image of his Son."* [31] No matter what we've done, no matter how many times we've done it, and no matter how long we've been away from him, Jesus is waiting for us and he longs for us to return to him. And he does this especially in the Sacrament of Reconciliation.

The second aspect of God's mercy is not as well-known: healing. Jesus doesn't just want to forgive our sins, he wants to get to the root of our sins—the wounds in our hearts, the bad habits we've formed, the hurts from our past, the dysfunctional ways we relate to others. Jesus doesn't just want to pardon us like a judge. He wants to heal us like a physician. He wants to transform our hearts. The same Jesus

---

[31] Pope St. John Paul II, homily, 17th World Youth Day Solemn Mass (Downsview Park, Toronto, July 28, 2002), https://w2.vatican.va/content/john-paul-ii/en/homilies/2002/documents/hf_jp-ii_hom_20020728_xvii-wyd.html.

who gave sight to the blind, made the lame walk and the dead live wants to heal us of our own spiritual blindness, give us strength where we feel paralyzed and unable to change, and breathe new life into those areas in our souls we sense have been dying.

Indeed, if the Church is the field hospital in the secular world, then we need to go to the wounded not just with the moral truth, but also with the medicine of mercy. Never take for granted the Good News of Christ's mercy: his forgiveness and his healing power. These basic pillars can be effective in piercing through the hardest of hearts, offering our relativist friends the hope they need to turn toward Jesus and his moral truth. They really can be forgiven. And they really can be changed.

Questions for Reflection/Discussion

1. Think of a time when someone confronted you about something you were doing that was wrong. Maybe it was a boss or colleague addressing something about your work. Maybe it was a teacher, coach, or parent pointing out a mistake. Maybe it was a friend or spouse expressing how you were doing something that was hurting them. How did that make you feel? If you were inspired by them to change, what about their approach did you find encouraging? If you were crushed or discouraged by their approach, what do you think they could have done differently?

2. Pope Francis said many in the modern world are wounded. How are they wounded? How does this affect the way we share moral truth with them?

3. In sharing moral truth with others, why is it so important to lead with mercy? What happens when we tell others the truth but without the good news of God's mercy?

4. God's mercy is not just about forgiveness, but also healing. Imagine Jesus coming before you today and asking you what he asked a paralyzed man two thousand years ago: "Do you want to be healed?" (Jn 5:6). How would you respond? What weakness would you want him to heal the most? Take time in prayer to ask Jesus to help you in this area.

5. Pope St. John Paul II was quoted as saying, "We are not the sum of our weaknesses and failures; we are the sum of the Father's love for us and our real capacity to become the image of his Son." Do you sometimes view yourself as the sum of your weaknesses? How do St. John Paul II's words encourage you to see yourself the way God sees you? How would this be good news for your friends who live a life far removed from the moral law?

Key Two

"Relativism Wounds People"

If we want to be effective in our conversations about moral truth, we must show our friends what's really at stake. Too often, moral topics are discussed as abstract concepts to be debated in a classroom or personal opinions that don't affect the real world. But in reality, how we think about these important matters has a tremendous impact on how we live. Indeed, people's lives are at stake. The Christian and relativistic worldviews are not just two very different philosophies. They lead to two very different ways of life— and we need to show the contrasts as clearly as possible.

This is one main reason the early Christians transformed ancient Rome: they persuasively revealed the emptiness of the mainstream, decadent lifestyles of the Roman world and demonstrated the joy and happiness found in following Christ. Joseph Ratzinger (Pope Emeritus Benedict XVI) explained that we need to do the same in our present era: "Today it is a matter of the greatest urgency to show a Christian model of life that offers a livable alternative to the increasingly vacuous entertainments of leisure-time society." [32]

---

[32] Joseph Ratzinger and Marcello Pera, *Without Roots: The West, Relativism, Christianity, Islam*, trans. Michael F. Moore (New York: Basic Books, 2006), 125.

And this is our second key to responding to relativism: *Spell out the sharp contrasts between the two worldviews* and help people to see what Pope Francis has observed: *"Relativism wounds people."*[33] If people stopped and truly considered the kind of life relativism leads to, most would probably reject it outright. But if you contrast the relativistic perspective with the joy, authentic love, and sense of purpose that flows from the classical worldview, the Christian way of life is convincingly more attractive than anything relativism has to offer. We just need to do a better job of highlighting the differences. To that end, let's consider four major contrasts between these worldviews and how they dramatically impact the way we live. The four differences are centered on how each perspective views (1) life's purpose, (2) relationships, (3) a good life, and (4) freedom.

In the end, we will see that relativism is not just a bad idea; in the words of Pope Francis, it is "the spiritual poverty of our time"[34]—and one that is severely wounding people's lives.

1. Life: A Story or No Plot?

"Whether I shall turn out to be the hero of my own life ... these pages must show."[35]

This first line of Charles Dickens's novel, *David Copperfield*, expresses one key feature of a Catholic moral worldview: life is a story. Western Civilization has traditionally viewed

---

[33] Pope Francis, *The Name of God is Mercy*, 15. Emphasis added.

[34] Pope Francis, address, Audience with the Diplomatic Corps Accredited to the Holy See (Sala Regia, March 22, 2013), http://w2.vatican.va/content/francesco/en/speeches/2013/march/documents/papa-francesco_20130322_corpo-diplomatico.html.

[35] Charles Dickens, *David Copperfield* (Oxford: Oxford University Press, 1999), 1.

human life as taking on a narrative shape. There is a plot to everyone's life, and we are like characters striving together toward a goal. Each person has a role to play and, deep down, we each desire to play it well. We hope to be the hero of our own lives.

Where is the drama of our life story played out? Where are we each called to such heroism? For most of us, this will probably not happen on the battlefield, a sports stadium, or the political stage, but in the way we live our most fundamental relationships on a daily basis. Will we live a successful life with our spouse, our children, our parents, our friends, our neighbors, and our God? That's the crucial question that defines every human life, for each human person is made for friendship.

Living Like Frodo

To better understand the narrative form of life, let's consider the main character in J. R. R. Tolkien's well-known saga *The Lord of the Rings*: Frodo the Hobbit. In the story, Frodo is entrusted with a perilous mission to destroy the Ring of Power that threatens Middle Earth if it is discovered by the evil demonic figure, Sauron. Moment by moment, Frodo is making decisions that lead him either closer to his goal of destroying the evil Ring, or further away from his goal and thus threatening to end up a tragic failure. Every day, the way Frodo lives his life matters. When he acts with courage,

> Every day I make choices that make me either a more or a less loving husband to my wife; a better or a worse father to my kids; a better or weaker son of God.

patience, or prudence, he becomes more like a hero as he advances toward completing his quest. But when he acts out of fear, makes rash decisions, or uses the Ring, he puts the entire mission in jeopardy.

So we see that many others in Middle Earth are dependent on Frodo. His life matters. His choices matter. What he decides to do with his life is not simply a "personal choice." The way he lives his life step-by-step will affect many other people.

Similarly, we need to see our own lives in a narrative framework. Like Frodo, every day we are making decisions that affect our life story—choices that either lead us closer to or further away from our goal of becoming the kind of person we hope to be. Every day, therefore, I am making decisions that make me more of a hero or more of a failure in my home. Every day I make choices that make me either a more or a less loving husband to my wife; a better or a worse father to my kids; a better or a worse teacher to my students; a better or a weaker son of God.

As with Frodo, how I live my life will deeply impact other people—for better or for worse. Other people will be affected by the choices I make each day. My life, therefore, matters. My choices matter. Will I be the hero of my life? Only the choices I make each day will tell.

The Larger Story

Most importantly, we must view each individual life not as its own isolated story, but rather within the context of a much larger story about the human family as a whole—the epic drama that spans back to the beginning of time. It is the story of the battle between good and evil, between God and the devil, between the woman and the serpent. St. Augustine described it as the strife between the City of God and the

City of Man.[36] Pope St. John Paul II more recently described it as a conflict between the "civilization of love" and the "culture of death."[37]

Each person has a role to play in this struggle. Indeed, each life will either serve God's kingdom and help overcome evil, or it will assist Satan in extending his domain in the world. Throughout the centuries, others have come in and out of this grand story and played their part for better or worse: Adam and Eve, Cain and Abel, David and Saul in the Old Testament, and Peter and Paul or Judas and Pilate in the New Testament. There have been many martyrs and their wicked persecutors, such as Pope Sixtus II and the Emperor Valerian, or St. Thomas More and King Henry VIII. And in times of crisis there have been those who have stood out as courageous witnesses to the truth, and others who compromised their faith either because they stubbornly wanted to conform to this world or were too apathetic or afraid to resist its ways.

We stand in this line of many great saints and martyrs as well as cowards and villains who have gone before us. Now it is our turn to step into the story. How well will we play our part? Will our small lives help bring life to the world, building up God's Kingdom and a Civilization of Love? Or will we follow the selfish, individualistic ways of modern living and contribute to the Culture of Death? In other words, will you be the hero of your life? The choices you make each day in your relationships will show.

---

[36] See: St. Augustine, *The City of God.*
[37] John Paul II, *Evangelium Vitae* ("The Gospel of Life"), 12.

Relativism: Your Life Has No Meaning

Part of the problem we face is that the modern relativistic world has taken away our story. Instead of imparting identity and mission to each new generation by showing them their crucial role in the story, relativism denies that there is an overarching narrative to the human family in which each person finds his purpose and meaning. Rather, each individual makes up his own story. He doesn't have a role to play in some imaginary Christian narrative about good and evil. For the relativist, there *is* no good and evil. Since, therefore, there are no right or wrong choices, your decisions, in the end, do not matter.

> Imagine if the world of *Lord of the Rings* were a relativistic world ... It would not matter what Frodo does with his life.

But this is a very shallow view of life. Ultimately, relativism is saying that your life has no significance. Your life has no meaning or purpose. What you choose to do with your life simply does not matter. Imagine if the world of *Lord of the Rings* were a relativistic world—a world in which there was no right or wrong. In such a world, it would not matter what Frodo does with his life. Whether he destroys the Ring, uses it for his own personal gain, or hands it to the dark lord Sauron does not matter. All that matters is that Frodo is free to choose.

Would this be a stimulating book or entertaining movie? Not at all! If there is no meaning in Frodo's choices, *Lord of the Rings* would become a very dull story. A good story needs a plot—and that is exactly what is missing when relativism reigns and choices no longer matter. Similarly, we human beings need a plot for our lives. We need to have a sense that our lives have a purpose and that our choices matter. But that is precisely what the relativistic perspective excludes. It is no wonder many people today fear that their lives are going nowhere. In our individualistic culture that takes away the real plot to our lives, people are told to do whatever they want; as a result, many begin to doubt whether their lives have real meaning.

But for a human being to lose the narrative thread of his life is dangerous. Think of what happens when we encounter a boring story. If we watch a movie that is going nowhere, we turn it off. When we read a book without a plot, we set it down. And when people sense that their lives lack purpose and meaning, they turn them off in various tragic ways. Some people fall into depression. Others become workaholics, constantly busying themselves because it is easier to keep up a flurry of activity than to face the emptiness in their hearts. Still others fill their souls with the constant distracting noise and images from movies, the Internet, social media, and pointless videos because they fear being alone with their own thoughts. This attempt to escape meaninglessness also manifests itself in addictions to alcohol, drugs, pornography, and sex.

Some people even turn their lives off quite literally through suicide—an increasing problem in the world, which often is rooted in failing to see one's life in a narrative framework. In the case of people contemplating suicide, William Kilpatrick writes:

> The problem is not so much that they have lost their self-esteem (although that is certainly part of it) but, more important that they have lost the narrative thread of their lives. Life itself has become pointless, without plot or direction. We are willing to endure suffering when the suffering has meaning, but meaning is exactly

what is absent in the case of a potential suicide. When suffering
can be set within a narrative scheme, we manage to keep going; but
if life itself is pointless, why put up with its thousand mockeries
and cruelties?[38]

Thus relativism is more than just a bad idea. By taking away
our story, it actually has the power to ruin people's lives.

2. Relationships: Commitment or Use?

A second major difference between the classical and
relativistic worldviews lies in how each understands
relationships. In the classical vision, every human person is
made for relationship—friendship with God and the people
God has placed in our lives. It is in these relationships that
we find our fulfillment. We're wired this way. We're made
for self-giving love. As Ratzinger explained: "Man lives in
relationships, and the ultimate goodness of his life depends
on the rightness of his essential relationships—I mean father,
mother, brother, sister, and so forth—the basic relationships
that are inscribed in his being."[39]

Our relativistic world, however, teaches just the opposite.
Life is *not* about our relationships. The self is viewed as an
autonomous individual, an island, separate from others.
Our most fundamental relationships—with God, parents,
siblings, spouse, children, friends, and community—are not
an essential part of who we are. The self is simply a blank
slate, and there are no right or wrong ways to approach our
relationships. In this outlook, we find fulfillment in life *not*
by giving ourselves to others, but by detaching ourselves
from others so we can be free to do whatever *we* want. We

---

[38]   Kilpatrick, *Why Johnny Can't Tell Right from Wrong*, 194.
[39]   Ratzinger, *Salt of the Earth*, 22.

tend to keep people as a part of our lives only to the extent that we get something out of them.

Feeling Alone

This relativistic outlook dramatically affects our relationships. It gets us to treat people like products. We value them in a utilitarian way—only insofar as they give us some benefit. As a result, relationships involving long-term, unconditional, sacrificial love are not as common as they used to be. In a relativistic world, our relationships become more self-serving and thus more unstable and tentative.

We feel this. We feel this instability in our families, in our dating relationships, in our friendships, and in our jobs. Deep down, we know that some people in our lives are not really committed to us as persons—they don't love us for our own sake. They're just in it for themselves. They are committed not to us, but to what they get out of us: good times, feelings, productivity, enjoyment, or advantage. But what happens when the feelings fade, the fun times wane, and we're no longer advantageous for them to know? Will they still be there for us? In our hearts, we know they probably won't. So we live in constant insecurity, uncertain what our boyfriend/girlfriend, spouse, boss, or friend will do as soon as we're no longer valuable to them or they can get what they're looking for somewhere else.

Thus, friendships constantly change. Dating relationships are fraught with insecurity. We live in greater isolation as no one is truly committed to us and no one knows us for who we really are. It is no wonder more and more people experience the pains of loneliness. The percentage of Americans who said they had no close personal friends (defined as someone with whom they could confide personal matters) increased dramatically from 10% in 1985 to almost 25% in 2004.[40] Think about that: about one out of every four people in our country does not have a close personal friend. Luigi Giussani, in his book *The Religious Sense*, describes how this instability has left people with a feeling of "relational seasickness":

> Uncertainty in relationships is one of the most terrible afflictions of our generation. It is difficult to become certain about relationships, even within the family. We live as if we were seasick, with such insecurity in the fabric of our relations that we no longer build what is human. We might construct skyscrapers, atomic bombs, the most subtle systems of philosophy, but we no longer build the human because it consists of relationships.[41]

Nowhere is this instability felt more than in marriage and family life. Marriage is no longer about husband and wife seeking what is best for each other and rallying around serving any children that may come from their union. Instead, love is reduced to feelings, and relationships are based on what the other person brings me: my beloved helps me, makes me feel good, brings me romantic feelings, or brings me pleasure. But if the marriage gets difficult and "you've lost that lovin' feeling," then it's better to back out of it and pursue something else that will be more interesting for you. After all, in a relativistic world, there's no good or bad way to live marriage. You can do whatever you want, whatever makes

"Uncertainty in relationships is one of the most terrible afflictions of our generation."
—Luigi Giussani

---

[40] Associated Press, "Lonely Nation", *CNN*, posted August 6, 2006, http://www.cnn.com/2006/HEALTH/07/31/lonely.nation.ap/index.html.

[41] Luigi Giussani, *The Religious Sense* (Montreal: McGill-Queen's University Press, 1997), 19.

you happy, regardless of how this might affect your spouse or children. We see once again that relativism is not just a bad idea. It wounds people. It puts the self at the center in such a way that our own interests become more important than the people God has placed in our lives.

3. What Is a Good Life?

If someone asked you, "Are you a good person?" how would you respond?

Many people would say, "Sure. I'm nice to people. I'm friendly. I work hard. I'm easy to get along with. I don't offend people. I guess that makes me a pretty good person." But let's step back and consider this question more closely. Does simply being nice and not hurting others make me a good person? *What does it actually mean to be a good person?*

We tend to say "he's a good person" without much reference to whether the man is virtuous, or fulfilling his *telos*, his purpose. Typically, the expression merely reflects a sentiment one has in regard to another person. For most people, the expression "He's a good man" simply means "He's a nice guy" or "I like him" or "He's fun to be around." But for the ancient philosopher Aristotle, the statement "He's a good man" has little to do with how we feel about someone or whether we like being around them. "He's a good man" is a statement of fact. It is a statement as factual as "This is a good watch." What makes a good watch? A good watch fulfills the purpose of a watch well: it tells time accurately. Just as a good pen writes well and a good harpist plays the harp well, something is described as good when it fulfills the *telos* for which it is made.

Thus, a man is declared to be good because he is fulfilling his *telos*. Since, as we've seen, man is made for relationships—relationship with God and neighbor—a good man is someone who lives his relationships with excellence. He possesses the virtues needed to live his relationships well. This has huge implications for how we see if we are on track in our own lives. If you want to evaluate whether you are a good person, you should ask yourself how well you are living out the most fundamental relationships in life:

- How well are you living out your relationship with your parents? With your siblings? Are you a good son/daughter or brother/sister to them?

- How well are you living out your relationship with your spouse and kids? Are you a good husband/wife and a good father/mother?

- Are you a good friend, colleague, neighbor, citizen?

- Most of all, how well are you living your relationship with God right now?

These are the questions that get to the heart of what kind of person you are. If we're honest, most of us recognize we fall short of where we'd like to be in these relationships. Remember the funeral example from chapter 2: Which qualities do you want to be remembered for when your life on earth has ended? That question got us to think about the kind of person we want to be and the areas we need to grow in order to get there. Unless we're saints, most of us have not reached perfection yet. That doesn't mean we're horrible people—but it reminds us that we are still works in progress. And, of course, we don't have full control over relationships—others may do certain things that prevent the relationship from growing. But we want to ask honestly if we are doing the best we can to give of ourselves. For in the end, being a good person is not just about being nice. A good man, for example, is a good son to his parents, a good brother to his siblings, a good husband to his wife, a good father to his children, a good friend to his friends, a good worker for his employer, a good citizen contributing to his community.

Relativism, however, offers a very different outlook on life. A good life has nothing to do with our relationships. A good life is simply one in which a person decides for himself what he wants to do. Instead of training people to be a good son, brother, husband, father, friend, citizen, and son of God, the relativistic world simply teaches children, "Be yourself. Be your own person.... Become whoever you want to be." We tell young people they can do anything they want to do, but we don't form them in the virtues they need to live out relationships of sustained commitment—the very relationships where they will find their happiness.

> A good man, is a good son to his parents, a good husband to his wife, a good father to his children, a good friend to his friends.

4. Freedom: For Love or for License?

At the center of the differences between the classical and relativistic worldviews is the understanding of freedom. We've seen how in the classical view freedom is the ability to perform actions of high quality. It's *for* something. If I possess the skills of violin playing, I'm free to play the violin with excellence. Similarly, if I possess the life skills known as the virtues, I am free to give the best of myself in my relationships and thus find my happiness. Virtue gives me the freedom to love.

But we saw how the modern notion of freedom is self-centered. It's simply the ability to make choices. It's merely about being free from governments, religions, families, and others controlling me. How I choose to use my freedom, however, doesn't matter. There are no good or bad choices. All that's important is that I choose. It's about the license to do what I want and being free from anyone telling me what to do.

A Tale of Two Marriages

A true story about two married couples who lived in the same neighborhood at the same time highlights the stark difference between these two views of freedom. One young couple had been happily married for several years with two children when the wife was diagnosed with terminal cancer. She quickly lost the ability to walk and knew she'd be in a wheelchair for the remainder of her life. This wasn't what her husband was expecting when they got married. The emotional and financial pressure was too much. He wanted a different kind of life. So in the middle of her battle with cancer, he left his wife and kids for another woman. According to the modern view of freedom, we can't say what he did was wrong. Maybe you wouldn't do that, but we should celebrate that he's free to do whatever he wants. And if he wants to leave his dying wife and his kids, that's his decision.

Just blocks away, however, lived another couple. The wife was diagnosed with an aggressive form of multiple sclerosis. She also quickly lost mobility and had to be pushed in a wheelchair for the rest of her life, but her situation was even more incapacitating. She couldn't bathe, clothe, or feed herself. She couldn't even speak. Her husband was just hitting his stride in his business but decided to retire early so that he could take care of his slowly dying wife. He went through practically all of his savings, fully realizing that he would not have much left for himself in his golden years. But that didn't matter. He lovingly poured his life out for his wife in her remaining years, feeding her, bathing her, dressing her, and serving her every need. Each day he'd take his wife outside for walks in the neighborhood. He constantly read to her and talked to her, telling her about the weather, their friends and family, what was happening in the world, her favorite baseball team—even though she could not say a single word back. For years, he never had even one conversation with the love of his life. But he was always by her side, all the way to the end. Indeed, his virtuous character shone all the more in these trying years, as he was still able, still *free*, to give the best of himself for his dying wife amid the most difficult of circumstances.

> Both husbands saw their life story take an unanticipated turn. One walked away from love and responsibility while the other revealed himself to be a hero.

The tale of these two couples encapsulates the main contrasts between the classical and relativistic worldviews. Both husbands saw their life story take an unanticipated turn. And at that pivotal moment, one walked away from love and responsibility while the other revealed himself to be a hero. One lived the kind of life we might expect an individualistic culture to produce. The other rose above the mainstream and reminds us of what true greatness is all about. His life was not about him—it was about giving himself to others, most especially his wife. What would you do if your character was tested in this way? Will you be the hero of your own life?

Questions for Reflection/Discussion

1. How is life a story? What difference does it make to see your daily decisions as part of a larger narrative?

2. This chapter discussed becoming the hero of our own lives. How do we become that hero in our life story? Where does that heroism take place? What distracts us from striving to be a hero in those things that matter most in life?

3. What might be the connection between relativism and the loneliness and instability many people experience in relationships today?

4. Pope Francis taught that "relativism wounds people." Do you think this is the case? Why or why not?

5. How might you articulate the differences in lifestyle that flow from the relativistic and classical worldviews?

Key Three

Law = Love

Law equals love. That's the third crucial point we need to keep in mind in our conversation with relativistic friends. No matter what moral issue we may be discussing, we always need to bring it back to love—and quickly. Otherwise, people likely won't take us seriously. They'll think that we're just imposing our own way of looking at the world on others. Even with good rational arguments in hand, we risk sounding more like a walking catechism than men and women with hearts. We need, therefore, to *reframe* the discussion if we're going to be effective. Morality, at its heart, is not about rules. It's about love. It comes from love. It leads us to love. And it's an act of love to share the moral path with others.

So whether we're talking about the environment, abortion, marriage, poverty, or sex, remember that we're ultimately talking about love. Do you want to love more? Do you want to be a loving person? Do you want to be loved? Do you want others to receive authentic love? Every moral issue, in the end, comes down to love.

This was made clear to me on a flight home after a speaking event on the East Coast. There was a man boarding the plane who had seen a film series on TV that I had been a part of.

He was going down the aisle heading toward his seat when he saw me. He stopped and asked:

"Are you Edward Sri? ... I've been watching *Symbolon* on the Catholic cable channel EWTN, and I'm learning so much! I love the show, and I'm not even Catholic—I'm a Methodist. I have some questions about the Catholic Faith. When we get up in the air, could we talk?"

I, of course, agreed, thinking to myself, "This is someone who enjoyed the show. And he's Methodist. He probably has some questions about Mary and the Bible, or Confession, or the Mass. It will be fun to help him out." Little did I know what I was getting myself into.

After our plane leveled off at 38,000 feet, he tapped me on the shoulder; I stood up to greet him and we began talking. The other travelers were immersed in reading or working on their laptops, oblivious to our theological conversation while standing in the aisle—until he dropped the bomb on me:

"So here's my big question: When is the Catholic Church finally going to update all of its teachings on sexuality?"

Immediately, everyone put down what they were doing and looked up at me, wondering how I'd respond. I, too, was wondering how I'd answer. But he didn't give me a chance.

> "So here's my big question: When is the Catholic Church finally going to update all of its teachings on sexuality?"

For several minutes, he pressed me on how all the other Christian denominations have gotten with the times; how the Catholic Church's teachings on sex are oppressive and inhumane; how people should be free to express love the way they want to; how the Church shouldn't be interfering with people's sexual lives; how the Church should be more open-minded. He was kind and sincere, but intense and relentless with his questions. Finally, I sensed I just needed to jump in and stop the tirade for a moment. "Excuse me," I said with a smile. "Do you know why the Catholic Church teaches what it does about sex? And do you know why it's *always* going to teach what it teaches about sex? *It's because the Catholic Church loves people!*" That's not what he was expecting.

"Let me ask you a question," I continued. "Do you work with young people? I am blessed to do so regularly. I work with thousands of college students and young adults around the country in various schools and ministries. And these young people are very familiar with the ideas you're describing—ideas from the sexual revolution. They've experienced first-hand the repercussions of these ideas which shape the world in which they grow up today. And they've told me how it's affected them.

"They've experienced casual sex, the hookup culture, free-flowing relationships. And it's not working for them. It has left them empty and wounded. They describe the fears and insecurities they have in dating relationships ... the pain and heartache in their lives ... how they have felt used ... how they have felt let down ... how they have become disillusioned. So many of them come from broken homes and have experienced the heartache of divorce. Many of them doubt they will ever find a lasting love. Is this what we want for the next generation?"

I also discussed with him how fewer and fewer people are getting married today. Many say to themselves, "Marriage? Why bother? I have a boyfriend/girlfriend. We like each other, we live together, and we have good jobs ... why do we need a certificate from some church?" Many of them have not seen strong marriages modeled in their own families and communities, and they themselves have gone from one hookup to another, and one dead-end relationship to another. So the very idea of a lifelong, joyful, and committed marriage does not even seem possible.

And yet—and this is utterly fascinating—the strong majority of adults in the United States still say that one of their main goals in life is to have a happy marriage.[42] How can that be? If so few people bother with marriage these days, why are so many still saying they hope to have a happy marriage? Because they are still human persons created with a desire for a lasting love. God made them for love, and they still desire love. They just don't think a lifelong love is possible, so they have given up on marriage. That's why we need to proclaim the good news of marriage: the desires young people have for total and committed love are good! And they can have their heart's deepest desires fulfilled if they follow God's plan for love, marriage, and sexuality, not the world's way.

> We need to frame each moral teaching within the context of love.

These are some of the ideas I quickly shared with my Methodist friend at 38,000 feet. Though I can't say I convinced him in our short conversation in the aisle, it did stop him and make him ponder the issue a little more. And sometimes that's the best we can do in an initial exchange. But the one thing that is crucial to do at an early stage is to *reframe the discussion.* Instead of letting our friends paint Catholic moral teaching as something negative—something

---

[42] Linda J. Waite and Maggie Gallagher, *The Case for Marriage* (New York: Broadway Books, 2000), 2–3.

interfering with people's personal lives—we need to frame each moral teaching within the context of love. For that's what all of Christ's moral teachings are about.

The moral law comes from God's love: He made us, he knows how we work, and he loves us so much he gives us the law to show us how to live in a way that will lead to our happiness. *And the moral law helps us grow in love.* These aren't just random rules from our religion. The moral law corresponds to how God made us and what he made us for. It's the instruction manual for our lives. So whatever the particular moral issue we might be discussing—whether it's about contraception, the environment, abortion, or immigration—we must always highlight how the moral law helps us to love.

Unfortunately, love is the last thing people think about when they hear about moral law. Morality is often viewed as just a long series of no's. But like many good things in life, smaller no's enable us to say yes to bigger things that are more important. An athlete says no to eating certain foods in order to be fit and excel at his sport. A mother says no to certain hobbies so she can have more time for her children. An engaged couple says no to dating other people because they are saying yes to building a life together in marriage. To be excellent in anything in life requires discipline and perseverance—little no's that create the space for a bigger yes. The same is true with morality.

Catholic social teaching, for example, doesn't condemn the unjust use of wealth and stop there. It challenges us to care personally for the poor and suffering in this world, to say "Yes" to loving them as persons, and to encounter them as brothers and sisters. And when we do that, we don't just have an impact on other people. Something changes within us. We become transformed by love. We become "persons moved by Christ's love, persons whose hearts Christ has conquered with his love, awakening within them a love of neighbor."[43]

Similarly, Christian teaching on human life isn't just about saying no to abortion and euthanasia. That's just a basic foundation, so that we actually get out of ourselves and say yes to caring for the weaker members of society, whether it be the elderly, the handicapped, or the unborn. We begin to see our elderly parents, a person with special needs, or the unborn child in the womb not as burdens or obstacles getting in the way of what we want to do in life. We begin to see them as persons, as brothers and sisters who need our care and attention, who invite us to "look them in the eye" and accompany them in life. And when we do that, something again changes within us. We grow in love.

Being able to make moves like this in our conversations with our relativistic friends requires that we do our homework. We need to understand particular moral issues better so we can effectively draw connections to love. Good books, articles, priests, and friends can help point us in the right direction whenever we're seeking to understand a certain topic better. But whenever learning about the moral teachings of the Church, always be thinking about how it relates to love. How does this help protect love or encourage greater love? In the end, if the moral law is understood properly, the real question should not be, "Do I really have to follow this law?" but rather, "Do I want to love? Do I want to love God and the people in my life as much as I can?

---

[43] Pope Benedict XVI, *Deus Caritas Est*, 33, (December 25, 2005), http://w2.vatican.va/content/benedict-xvi/en/encyclicals/documents/hf_ben-xvi_enc_20051225_deus-caritas-est.html

Because if I do, I should be grateful for God's law showing me the way of love."

So let's not be timid about presenting God's moral law. And let's never leave people with the impression that his law is some random rule or a restriction on freedom. Rather, the moral law comes from such a good King who loves us so much that he revealed to us the way of love. He wants us to be able to love and to be happy. May we joyfully radiate our confidence that the law is "a light to my path" and "a lamp to my feet" (Ps 119:105), calling us out of ourselves and calling us on to greater self-giving love and responsibility. *Law = love.*

Questions for Reflection/Discussion

1. Why do you think many people have a negative impression of moral laws? Why are they uncomfortable with the idea that there might be a right or wrong for everyone?

2. In your own words, explain how at the heart of God's moral law is love.

3. When you hear Christians talk about morality, do you think they leave the impression that law is about love? Why or why not?

4. Now, how about you: When a moral topic comes up with friends or family, how well do you demonstrate that love is at the center of God's moral law?

5. In these conversations, what would you want to avoid doing in the future? What could you do better?

Key Four

Making Judgments vs. Judging Souls

Our culture has accepted two huge lies. The first is that if you disagree with someone's lifestyle, you must fear or hate them. The second is that to love someone means you agree with everything they believe or do. Both are nonsense. You don't have to compromise conviction to be compassionate.[44]

This quote from Protestant pastor Rick Warren sums up a two-edged sword we face when talking about morality today. On one hand, if we say a certain behavior is wrong, people get angry because they automatically assume we're condemning them—that we hate them or think they're a bad person. "Don't judge me!" they say. On the other hand, if we don't joyfully accept other people's ideas or ways of living, we find ourselves judged and condemned for not being more tolerant and loving. "You don't approve of what I'm doing. That means you don't love me."

But let's take a closer look at this: Are we being hateful just because we think something is wrong? Can we make a judgment in our heads without judging a person's heart? This leads to our fourth key to engaging relativistic friends:

---

[44] Rick Warren, "What Must We Do?" in *Not Just Good, but Beautiful*, ed. Steven Lopes and Helen Alvaré (Walden, NY: Plough Publishing House, 2015) 104.

to underscore the *big difference between making a judgment and judging a person's soul.*

Making a Judgment vs. Judging Souls

Is it okay for me to use my mind and simply make a judgment? If I notice it's raining, I make a judgment: "I should bring my umbrella." If it's snowing, I make a judgment: "I should wear my winter coat." Am I a mean, bigoted person if I do this? Of course not. God gave me a mind. He wants me to use it.

Similarly, can I use my mind to make a judgment about someone else's actions? If I see my toddler about to run into the street, can I make the judgment "That's not good for her. She might get hit by a car"? Or if I see her about to touch a hot burner on the stove, can I use my mind and make the judgment, "That's not good for her. She will get burned." If I do this, I'm not saying she's a horrible person. I'm just observing that she is about to do something that will cause her great harm.

Let's take this a step further. Can I use my mind and make a judgment about someone else's *moral* actions? Let's say there's a young female college student who is sleeping around with one man after another each week. Can I use my mind and make the judgment, "That's not good for her"? Can I make the judgment, "She's not going to be happy living this way. She's never going to find the lasting love she longs for"? Of course.

But let's be clear: I'm not judging her *soul* if I do that. She may be doing something objectively wrong, but I don't know her personal situation before God. I don't know her background, her situation, or her intentions. Who am I to judge? A soul's status before God is something between that person and God alone. Various factors in people's lives may impair their free choices in such a way that limits their culpability or moral guilt.[45] As Pope Francis explains, "Each person's situation before God and their life in grace are mysteries which no one can fully know from without."[46] Perhaps this young woman has never experienced authentic love. Maybe she was sexually abused. Maybe she has always been taught that this is what it means to be a liberated woman. Such a woman needs to know my compassion, not just a lecture on the moral law.

At the same time—and this is absolutely crucial—if I care about her at all, should I say something to her about what she's doing? If she is a close friend or family member, for example, should I talk to her about it? I wouldn't be judging her soul—that's between her and God alone. But to love is to will the good of another, to seek what's best for the other person. And if I truly love this person, then it's the loving thing to show her the better way.

> "Each person's situation before God and their life in grace are mysteries which no one can fully know from without."
>
> —Pope Francis

Certainly I should do this prudently, in the right time and in the right way, and with great gentleness, humility, and compassion. But it is *not* loving to sit back and never want to share the truth with her.

Imagine if I see my two-year-old daughter about to touch the hot stove and I say to myself, "Well, I wouldn't do that. But I don't want to be judgmental. Whatever makes her happy. ... " Or imagine if my toddler is about to run into the street and I say to her, "Oh well ... if that works for you! ...

---

[45] See *Catechism of the Catholic Church* 1735.
[46] Pope Francis, *Evangelii Gaudium* ("The Joy of the Gospel"), 172.

I personally wouldn't do that, but I don't want to impose my views on you. It's your life. Let's just coexist." Would that be a loving thing to do? Absolutely not.

The Two Sides of Love

One of the most successful worldwide organizations to help people struggling with alcoholism is Alcoholics Anonymous. When advising families that have a loved one struggling with alcoholism, does AA encourage them to say nothing—to just be tolerant and never bring the topic up? No. They urge the family to do an intervention. Family members should meet with the loved one and address the problem in a loving but firm and direct way: "Uncle Billy, we love you, and we see what you're doing to yourself. It's affecting you. And we see how it's hurting Aunt Sally. And it's hurting us, too." This is love: to will the good of another. Sitting back and saying nothing, however, is not the loving thing to do. Indifference does not equal love.

Yet this is what relativism forces us to do. It divides us. It trains us to focus on ourselves and ignore the people around us—what they're going through, how they're living, and ways they might need our help. When we see someone making poor choices, whether they are hurting themselves or hurting others, we should try to help them. But relativism confuses us. It makes us doubt ourselves ("Maybe it's not a big deal if he wants to get drunk all the time. He hasn't become physically abusive yet"). We wonder if it's our place to say anything ("I'm worried about my sister's relationship with her husband, but it's her life. I don't want to interfere"). We're also scared we'll be misunderstood if we intervene ("They'll think that I hate them, so I'm not going to say anything"). In many subtle ways, relativism paralyzes us. So we sit back and do nothing, and let our friends and relatives damage their lives.

Ultimately, relativism trains us to be indifferent to other people. We'll be polite and nice to others who are making bad choices. We might tolerate their decisions and "coexist" with them. *But do we love them?* In the end, relativism encourages us to be unconcerned about the people around us and neglect our responsibilities toward them. We become like Cain in the Bible, who when asked about the whereabouts of his brother, replied, "Am I my brother's keeper?" (Gn 4:9).

But that's not how Jesus lived. Jesus wasn't indifferent to others. He didn't say, "Well, it's not my life ... whatever works for them." No, Jesus came with two essential sides of love: a soft side of mercy, compassion, and acceptance, and a firm side that constantly calls us to conversion. On one hand, Jesus loved everyone, even in their sins and weaknesses. He came not to condemn and he taught us to do the same: "Judge not" (Mt 7:1). On the other hand, Jesus persistently challenged people to repent from the evil that they were doing. And he did this because he loved them and knew they would not be happy living apart from God's plan. We can see these two sides of love especially in the way Jesus treated the woman caught in adultery (cf. Jn 8:2–11). Jesus loved her even in her sin. But he also loved her too much to keep her there. What he said to her he says to all of us: Not just "Neither do I condemn you," but also "Go, and do not sin again."

> Relativism trains us to be indifferent to other people. We might tolerate their decisions and "coexist" with them. But do we love them?

Questions for Reflection/Discussion

1. Does "I disagree" mean "I hate you"? Does "I love you" mean "I agree with everything you believe and do"? Why or why not?

2. Have you ever experienced someone assuming you were judging them when you simply happened to disagree with them on some moral issue? If so, what happened? What do you think you could do better on your end to help dispel that false assumption?

3. In your own words, how would you explain the difference between making a judgment and judging a person's soul? How might this distinction be helpful in our conversations with relativist friends?

4. Why is it not loving to remain silent and to never intend to speak about moral truth with our friends?

5. How does relativism divide us, keeping us from loving the people in our lives?

Key Five

Relativism Is Not Neutral

One of the presumed benefits of moral relativism is that it promotes tolerance. We live in a pluralistic world, it is commonly said, and everybody has their own conception of right and wrong. Muslims, Jews, Buddhists, and Hindus each have their own beliefs about morality. So do secularists, capitalists, communists, environmentalists, feminists, and LGBT activists. Even among Christians, Fundamentalists and Evangelicals differ from mainstream Protestants, who in turn differ from the Catholic Church on a whole array of moral issues. In a world with so many competing claims to moral truth, how do we know who is right?

Relativists like to portray themselves as holding a neutral position. It's better to be open-minded toward *all* points of view, they say. Since we can't know truth, no one is right. No one is wrong. All groups can come together under the one big tent of relativism. Therefore, we should all get along and coexist.

At first glance, this seems like a good way to promote tolerance of diverse views. But we must understand very clearly that relativism, in fact, is *not* value neutral. Relativism itself is a certain way of looking at the world. And this view—that there is no right or wrong—is being imposed on us. In other words, the belief that there is no moral truth *is itself a point of view*. And those who do not agree with this relativistic perspective are being forced to play by its rules or risk being labeled as judgmental if they uphold traditional moral values.

Joseph Ratzinger once observed, "The more relativism becomes the generally accepted way of thinking, the more it tends toward intolerance, thereby becoming a new dogmatism ... It prescribes itself as the only way to think and speak—if, that is, one wishes to stay in fashion. Being faithful to traditional values and to the knowledge that upholds them is labeled intolerance, and relativism becomes the required norm." [47] He encourages us to push back: "I think it is vital that we oppose this imposition ... which threatens freedom of thought as well as freedom of religion." For relativism is "a kind of new 'denomination' that places restrictions on religious convictions and seeks to subordinate all religions to the super-dogma of relativism." [48]

> For relativism is "a kind of new 'denomination' that seeks to subordinate all religions to the super-dogma of relativism."
> —Joseph Ratzinger

This leads us to our fifth key to engaging moral relativism: *Show how relativism is not value neutral*. Relativism is not moral Switzerland. It is not a neutral, impartial, unbiased position. It is a point of view, a way of looking at the world, and we should not allow others to force this worldview upon us.

---

[47] Ratzinger, *Without Roots*, 128.
[48] Ibid.

Pushing Back

What do you do when your friend says to you, "Don't be so judgmental" or "Don't be so intolerant"? Some of us apologize, fearing we're offending someone. Others of us lose our cool. We get frustrated and angry. We try to prove we're right and they're wrong, using more arguments and more volume. Others of us just freeze. We feel a pit in our stomach and don't know what to say or do.

But what if the next time someone says to you, "Don't be so judgmental," you gently pushed back and asked, "Are you judging me?" Imagine the conversation going something like this:

Your Friend: Don't be so judgmental.

You: Excuse me. Are you judging me? I'm feeling judged right now. Are you saying I'm a judgmental person?

Your Friend: Uh, no ... I'm not quite saying that. ...

You: But you just told me not to be judgmental.

Your Friend: Well, when you say something is immoral, it sounds like you are judging others.

You: Look. You're free to believe whatever you want. If you want to believe there's no truth, no moral right or wrong, that's fine. I'll disagree with you, but I still respect you as a person. If you want to have faith in moral relativism and believe that there is no moral order to the universe, you're free to do that. But whatever you do, please do not impose your belief in no truth—your belief in relativism—on me! Please don't try to make me follow your religion of relativism!

Your Friend: (Silence)

You: Now, I have a question for you. Do you really believe that there is nothing *at all* that is morally wrong for everyone? How about murder? Rape? Genocide? ...

The benefit of this approach is that it quickly turns the conversation to a fundamental issue: Is there moral truth? Most discussions about morality remain on a heated personal and emotional level: "What are you saying about me? Who are you to judge? Who are you to say what's right and wrong?" Relativists aren't expecting a Christian to play their own "Don't Judge" trump card on them. And when that happens, it might get them to think about deeper issues. And you might have the chance to have a more rational conversation.

Remember, most people's relativism has not been well thought out. Now you can initiate a conversation that confronts the central issue of relativism: the assumption that each person decides for himself what's right or wrong. This hasn't been proven to you by your relativist friend. And it probably has not been proven to himself in his own head. It is usually only assumed and asserted because that's what's generally accepted in the culture. But now you have the opportunity to raise questions and challenge the relativistic assumptions by using some of the practical points we've been discussing.

Whatever you do, make sure you help your friend see that relativism is not automatically true for everyone just because that's his outlook. Show him how relativism is itself a certain way of looking at the world, *but it's not the only way.* Your friend probably has never heard of the key features of a classical worldview (as discussed in part one): virtue, authentic freedom, *telos*, friendship, love, law, grace, and happiness. Helping your friend get clarity on these fundamental topics will lay the foundation for him to think properly about specific moral issues. And over time, the inner unity of these various elements has more force than superficial, abstract arguments that don't address the more fundamental confusion your friend has about morality.

> Relativists aren't expecting a Christian to play their own "Don't Judge" trump card on them.

Indeed, the inner coherence of the classical worldview just makes sense. It makes sense out of life. And it makes sense out of people's personal experiences. Think about these basic points we considered in Part 2: We find our happiness in our relationships. We need virtue to live those relationships well. The virtues are the life skills that give us the freedom to love. Who can't agree with that? Having taught these ideas to thousands of college students and young adults for over twenty years, I have yet to hear anyone—whether Catholic, Protestant, Buddhist, feminist, homosexual, agnostic, or atheist—balk at any of these basic points. It resonates with their experiences and desires, and sheds light on their humanity.

Once these foundations are more or less accepted, we can begin to discuss the modern notion of freedom—the "I'm free to do whatever I want. It's my life" attitude—and ask them whether they think this mindset fosters or hinders our relationships. With your encouragement, most will admit that there are problems and recognize how this view supports selfishness and enables us to use others. And once the average person admits this, he is already more than halfway out of the hole of relativism. Individual topics will still need to be addressed, but moving the conversation to these fundamental matters is likely to bear more fruit than simply remaining at the level of, "Who are you to tell others what to do?"

Questions for Reflection/Discussion

1. Describe a time when you've been afraid to share the truth because you're afraid of being labeled intolerant or judgmental.

2. Joseph Ratzinger described how the more relativism is accepted, the more it becomes "a new dogmatism" and tends toward intolerance. Is that true? Do you think the relativistic culture is becoming ever more intolerant of other points of view?

3. In your own words, explain how relativism is not a neutral, totally open-minded position but a certain way of looking at life.

4. How would it be helpful in our conversations with friends to highlight that relativism is just one way of looking at the world, but not the only way?

5. This chapter suggested that the next time someone says to you, "Don't be so judgmental," you should respond by saying, "Are you judging me?" How might this approach be a helpful?

Key Six

Relativism Is a Mask

"So, Dr. Sri, do you think I'm a relativist?"

That was the odd question posed to me many years ago at a Catholic convention in the New York City area. I had just finished giving a presentation on moral relativism when an energetic young man chased me down through a crowd of conference attendees. He waved a spiral notebook in his hand and excitedly showed me the many pages of notes he took from the talk. He thanked me for the presentation, and then, in front of dozens of people, proceeded to ask his unusual, personal question.

"Your talk got me wondering if maybe *I'm* a relativist. What do you think?"

"Well, I don't really know you," I replied, unsure of how to answer. "But you're here at this Catholic conference. Are you a practicing Catholic?"

"Yes, I'm Catholic," he said. "I go to Mass, I go to Eucharistic Adoration, and I love going to conferences like these."

"Good. And do you believe all of the Church's teachings? Let's take one big moral issue today—do you think abortion is wrong?"

"Oh yes, abortion is definitely wrong for me."

There were those two small words—"for me." They sent up a red flag in my mind. I asked him about it.

"What do you mean by saying it's wrong *for you*? Don't you think abortion is wrong for *everyone*?" I asked.

"Well, I think abortion is terrible. I'm against it," he said. "But that's *my* truth. If someone else thinks abortion is okay, that's true for them. So, even though I don't like abortion, for them, I guess, it would be okay."

His answer made one thing very clear, and I told him so: "You *are* a relativist if you think that!" We then began a heated discussion about whether the baby in the womb is a baby in reality or just in his own personal opinion. But that did not get very far. The young man kept saying that "for him," the baby was an innocent human life but for others it might not be. So I changed the topic to address something more personal to him.

"You said you go to Mass and to Eucharistic Adoration. Do you believe Jesus is really present in the Eucharist?"

"Yes, I believe that. I like going to Adoration."

"Then what would you think of someone coming into a church and desecrating the Eucharist? Would that be morally bad?" I asked.

"Oh yes, for me, desecrating the Eucharist would be very bad."

There were those two little words again: "for me."

"What do you mean *for you*? Wouldn't it be a great moral evil if *anyone* desecrated the Eucharist?"

"I'd hate it if anyone did that. That would be terrible . . . but I'd think it's terrible because I'm Catholic and believe in the Real Presence. If someone were an atheist and didn't believe in the Eucharist, then, for them, it would not be bad."

The Two Towers

His response only intensified the conversation. I was appalled at what he was saying! Dozens more crowded around to hear the escalating debate. We were at a conference center in Newark, New Jersey, standing in a grand hallway with large windows looking out across the Hudson River toward Manhattan. It was only a couple years after the 9/11 terrorist attacks, so I pointed out the window and in a raised voice asked him,

> "Are you willing to go up to the kids who lost their mother or father in the World Trade Center and tell them that what the terrorists did was not wrong?"

"Are you really that much of a relativist? Really? Look out there! Just a few years ago, there were two towers standing there in Lower Manhattan, and terrorists flew airplanes into those buildings. Thousands of people died that day. Are you willing to go up to the kids who lost their mother or father in the World Trade Center, look them in the eye, and tell them that what the terrorists did was not wrong, because 'for them' they thought what they were doing was good? Could you really do that?"

He was startled by this scenario and nervously said, "Wow . . . that's . . . very personal. I lost friends in the towers that day. Oh, wow . . . That would be really hard . . . really hard. . . ." He continued stammering about what a horrible day 9/11 was. "It would be very, very difficult to do that—but, if I had to be honest, yes, I'd have to tell those kids that, for the terrorists, what they did was not wrong."

I couldn't believe what I was hearing. Here was a young man who was attending a Catholic conference and who loves

Eucharistic Adoration telling me that he could look children in the eye and tell them that the terrorists who killed their parents did not do anything wrong. At this point, I needed a big "Plan B."

In dismay, I replied, "I honestly don't know what more I can to say to you. But there's one thing you told me this evening I want to come back to. You said you love Jesus in the Eucharist. There's a Eucharistic Adoration chapel set up here for our conference. Let's go there together. I want you to go in front of Jesus in the Eucharist and prayerfully ask him what he thinks of your relativistic views. Ask Jesus if relativism is correct." He agreed to come. We knelt down in the chapel and said a short prayer together. He thanked me for the conversation and said he was going to stay and pray for a while. As I left him there, I noticed he got out his spiral notebook again and began writing.

Masking Other Issues

The next day, I was walking out of the closing Mass for the conference when the young man came rushing up to me, shouting, "Dr. Sri! Dr. Sri!" He flung out his spiral notebook again, showing me all the pages he wrote in the chapel the previous night. "I was there for hours writing and thinking about our conversation. I'm so glad I caught you before you left. I wanted to tell you something."

He caught his breath and slowed down his speech. "I realized last night that I'm not really a relativist. The only reason I've been trying to be one is that ... " He paused and looked at the ground before continuing. "The only reason I've been trying to be a relativist is that I want to be able to say that premarital sex is okay ... " Then he raised his head, looked me directly in the eye, and said, "I wanted to be able to say premarital sex is okay *for me.*"

What an honest, humble young man! I was so impressed by how he admitted to what was really lurking behind his relativistic positions. He had been trying to justify his own sexual behavior, and moral relativism was a convenient way to do so. By denying that there was an actual ethical standard everyone had to follow, he could ease his conscience and excuse himself for having premarital sex. Fortunately, this young man had the humility and the courage to recognize this and went on to express his desire to live a chaste life.

But not everyone has this humility. That's why we need to keep in mind a sixth key to engaging moral relativism: *Remember that relativism may be a mask covering up someone's own immoral behavior.* You may hear your friend talking about being nonjudgmental, being pro-choice, the definition of marriage, or some other issue in the culture for which we need greater tolerance. But the real issue driving his relativism might be something in his own moral life. It could be something from his past or something going on right now. It could be what he did to his girlfriend in high school or how he's treating his wife right now. It could be disregard for his parents, marital infidelity, contraception, or addiction to pornography. When people are quick to say that you shouldn't tell other people what's right and wrong, realize they might really be talking about themselves: "Be tolerant of *my* little sin; don't tell *me* what's right and wrong."

> "I wanted to be able to say that premarital sex is okay *for me.*"

Cognitive Dissonance

Psychologists point out that we human beings strive for internal consistency in our beliefs and our actions. We become psychologically uncomfortable when there's dissonance between what we believe and what we do. We're not at peace with ourselves. So when we do something that doesn't match up with our beliefs and values, we have two options: either we *change our behavior* to align with our beliefs, or we *change our beliefs* to line up with our behavior. And since it's easier to change our beliefs than change our behavior, many people are prone to find some way to rationalize their actions—to convince themselves that what they are doing is really okay.

> If I'm not willing to change my behavior to conform to God's moral law, relativism is an attractive option.

If, for example, I want to eat healthier and believe I should avoid consuming fried foods, what happens when I can't resist those crispy onion rings presented to me at a restaurant? I'll experience some inner turmoil. Part of me is uncomfortable with eating the onion rings because of the healthy eating commitment I just made. So I need to justify it somehow: I tell myself it's not that bad. Or I'm only eating them this one time. Or that if I eat a salad afterward, that will somehow make up for it. Onions are vegetables, after all, so onion rings can't be that bad. Since it's easier to change our thoughts than change our behavior, we typically find some way to rationalize our actions. The same is true in moral matters. Deep down, we know some actions are wrong. But when we do them anyway, we're not at peace. We have a guilty conscience. Now we have a critical choice to make: Will we admit we did something wrong and try to be better next time? Will we strive to change our behavior to conform to what we know to be good? Or will we willfully persist in doing what we know to be wrong?

If we chose the latter route, we'll likely start to change our beliefs in order to silence the voice of our conscience and convince ourselves that we're still good people. We do this in various dysfunctional ways. We *blame* other people for our behavior ("My boss doesn't understand." "My spouse started this." "If I hadn't been treated this way, I wouldn't be doing this."). We *make excuses* for ourselves ("I'm under a lot of pressure." "I'm not as bad as most people." "I only do this once in a while.") We *rationalize* what we're doing ("I'm not killing anybody or robbing a bank." "I'm not hurting anyone." "Many other people do this."). We also *distract* ourselves, keeping ourselves constantly busy and entertained, so we don't ever have to stop and think about our lives: where we've been, where we're going, or who we are becoming. We keep up the blaming, excuses, rationalizing, and distractions ... anything to keep us from thinking about what we're really doing.

This is where relativism comes in handy. If I'm not willing to change my behavior to conform to God's moral law, relativism is an attractive option. Whatever sin a person may be falling into, it is easier to be a relativist and say each individual can make up his or her own morality than it is to change the way one lives and give up those immoral ways. This recalls what Ratzinger once taught about "the dictatorship of relativism." "Today," he said, "we are building a dictatorship of relativism that does not recognize anything as definitive and whose ultimate goal consists solely of one's own ego and desires."[49] According to Ratzinger, the primary dictator in the relativistic outlook is one's own selfish desires. As such,

---

[49] Joseph Cardinal Ratzinger, Homily, Mass for the Election of the Supreme Pontiff.

relativism often serves as a mask to cover up one's selfishness or rationalize a particular sin. If there's a certain behavior that deep down one knows is wrong but doesn't want to change, moral relativism is a very attractive viewpoint because it liberates the person from having to follow any moral standard!

So we should realize that a lot more may be going on with our friends than what we see on the surface. Practically, keep in mind two main points. First, always pray for the issue behind the issue. You might be debating *X*, *Y*, or *Z*, but realize that the real issue might actually be a certain problem in your friend's own moral life. This may not always be the case, but praying and fasting for your friend is always beneficial. And it will be particularly helpful if your friend is, in fact, embracing relativism to mask a certain sin problem.

Second, be aware that using relativism to cover up a sin will never bring lasting peace to your friend's soul. No matter how confident and happy he appears on the outside, remember that all human persons are made for God. And when they don't live according to God's plan, they are uneasy. They have to keep up a pretense, constantly distracting themselves, and tirelessly convincing themselves that they aren't doing anything wrong. But God wants to take that burden away. All your friend has to do is throw himself in the arms of God's mercy. This is why leading with mercy in our conversations is so important (see Key 1). If your friend admits the truth of his own sinful actions, he can be forgiven and start anew. But his heart will be restless until it rests in the truth and love of God.

Questions for Reflection/Discussion

1. Tell about a time you rationalized something that deep down you know you shouldn't have done—an unnecessary purchase, an extra dessert you ate, something you said, your tone of voice, the way you treated someone. How did you handle the guilty feeling? What did you do to try to make it go away?

2. In the Biblical account of the first sin, God confronted Adam and Eve with what they did and gave them a chance to admit their fault. First, consider Adam's response: "The woman whom you gave to be with me, she gave me fruit of the tree, and I ate" (Gen 3:12). How well does Adam accept responsibility for his actions? Next, consider Eve's response to God: "The serpent beguiled me, and I ate" (Gen 3:13). How well does she admit her fault?

3. In what ways might we, like Adam and Eve, tend to avoid admitting our faults and sins?

4. How might relativism be a convenient way for people to rationalize their sins?

5. This chapter discussed how when we're conversing with relativist friends about a certain moral topic, we should always pray for "the issue behind the issue." What does that mean? How might this change your approach with them?

Key Seven

Taking on the Heart of Christ

When we notice someone's faults, we are often quick to criticize and categorize the person in our heads— "Hmmm ... That's the third week in a row he didn't go to church," "Well, *she* was in a mood today!" "They're living together outside of marriage," "I can't believe he voted for *that* political candidate." Instead of our hearts being filled with patience, compassion, and mercy, we set ourselves up in judgment over our neighbor. And that's very dangerous, because while we may see certain facts, we don't always see the whole story.

There once was a young professional named Sarah who joined a Catholic women's group with her friends from work. They met each week for prayer, study, and fellowship. She was the only woman in the group who was no longer practicing her faith as a Catholic. But she felt very welcomed, liked the friendships, and enjoyed learning about the Bible and the Catholic Faith even though she wasn't going to Mass anymore.

Then one week, the subject of Confession came up. Sarah appeared uncomfortable. She was normally outgoing and contributing to the conversation, but during this discussion, she sat with her arms crossed, looking down without saying a word. When the study was over, she said she had to leave and didn't stay for the usual hangout time that followed. The leader of the small group felt horrible. She and the other women went out of their way to make Sarah feel welcomed, to be her friend, and not to pressure her with questions about why she wasn't going to Mass. The leader wondered, "Did I say something wrong? Did I offend her in some way?"

But the next day, Sarah gave the leader a call. "I'm sorry I left so abruptly last night. I'm sure everyone was wondering what was going on. I have to be honest—the topic of Confession hit me hard. I haven't been to Confession in ages … I haven't even stepped foot in a Catholic church since high school. The last time I went to Mass was at my father's funeral. … "

"All these years I haven't been able to forgive God for taking away my dad. That's why I haven't wanted to go to church . . . But I think I'm ready now. I think I want to set things right with God. You mentioned they have Confessions at the parish nearby. Do you know when?"

"They have Confession every Saturday morning," the small group leader replied.

"I've really appreciated our group," Sarah said. "You've all been so kind and patient with me. I think God is using you all to help me. I want to go to Confession and come back to the Church. Do you think you and the other women in our group would be willing to come with me Saturday morning, just to be nearby when I go to Confession? That would mean a lot to me."

From the outside we see only certain facts: a young Catholic woman no longer going to Mass. But when we learn the larger story of her life, instead of just making the legal observation ("She's missing the Sunday obligation!"), our hearts are full of compassion and greater understanding. Missing Mass is a problem. But when we see the bigger picture, we begin to view her situation the way God does: with gentleness and mercy.

It's dangerous to judge a person's status before God. As we saw in Key 4, various factors may impair people's free choices in such a way that limits one's culpability and moral guilt. As Pope Francis explains, "each person's situation before God and their life in grace are mysteries which no one can fully know from without." [50] Often we are not aware of the sufferings people go through that make it very difficult to live virtuously. People who have suffered, for example, from illness, hurts from their past, addictions, abuse, or psychological disorders, may be praiseworthy in God's eyes, even though they struggle with many faults. We often notice when they stumble, but we don't see the tremendous effort on the inside and the small gains they've made when we're not around.

That's why St. Therese of Lisieux emphasized that we should always respond to people's faults with charity, "for very often what we think is negligence is heroic in God's eyes. A sister who is suffering from migraine, or is troubled internally, does more when she does half of what is required of her than another who does it all, but is sound in mind and body." [51] There was one sister in her convent who had a rough personality and was particularly difficult to live with. Therese said, "I assure you that I have the greatest compassion for Sister X. If you knew her as well as I do, you would see that she is not responsible for all the things that seem so awful

---

[50] Pope Francis, *Evangelii Gaudium* ("The Joy of the Gospel"), 172.
[51] Genevieve of St. Teresa, testimony during the process of beatification, in *St. Therese of Lisieux: By Those Who Knew Her*, Christopher O'Mahony, ed. (Dublin: Veritas Publications, 1975), 132.

to us. I remind myself that if I had an infirmity such as hers, and so defective a spirit, I would not do any better than she does, and then I would despair; she suffers terribly." [52]

"Be Merciful. ... "

Jesus commands us to take on the heart of God the Father: "Be merciful, even as your Father is merciful" (Lk 6:36). The Bible describes our God as "merciful and gracious, slow to anger and abounding in mercy" (Ps 103:8). Do we reflect the kindness and mercy of God? Without in any way approving of sinful behavior, Jesus challenges us to examine whether our hearts are full of compassion for those whose lives are not perfect: Do we have an endless desire to show mercy? Or are we quick to criticize and condemn?

St. Catherine of Siena was once confronted by God about a hidden sin she had: the sin of judging people. She used to think that she had a gift for reading human nature and noticing other people's faults. But one day, God pointed out to her that the insights she was receiving about other people's weaknesses were not coming from him—they were coming from the devil! She came to see this was the devil's trap. The devil allows us to see other's faults, so that instead of wanting to help, we start to judge and condemn. Catherine admitted this to God, saying "You gave me ... as medicine against a hidden sickness I had not recognized, by teaching me that I can never sit in judgment on any person. ... For I, blind and weak as I was from this sickness have often judged others under the pretext of working for your honor and their salvation."[53]

---

[52] Sr. Agnes of Jesus, O.C.D., Ibid., 50-51.
[53] Catherine of Siena, *The Dialogue*, no. 108, trans. Suzanne Noffke, O.P. (New York: Paulist Press, 1980), 202.

Fellow Sufferers

If we face the truth about ourselves and experience our own daily struggles with sin, we are less likely to set ourselves up in judgment over others. If we recognize how much we need God's mercy—if we experience his forgiveness and saving power in our own lives—then our hearts will be much more compassionate when we encounter other people's faults. Truly experiencing God's patience and gentleness with our own weaknesses softens our hearts. It makes us more merciful toward others. That's why St. Catherine taught that when we notice a person's faults, we should say to ourselves, "Today it is your turn; tomorrow it will be mine unless divine grace holds me up."[54]

> "Today it is your turn; tomorrow it will be mine unless divine grace holds me up."
> —St. Catherine of Siena

But if we tend to respond to others' faults with condemnation, it may be because *we ourselves* have a serious moral problem. It could be because we have not come to terms with our own weakness and sins and have not really encountered God's mercy. It's not enough to simply *say* we are sinners who need forgiveness. The true disciple of Jesus knows this profoundly at the core of his being. He knows how selfish, proud, lazy, or fearful he really is—how much he fails to love. How about you? Do you feel the weight of how weak you really are and how utterly dependent you are on God's grace? Such a person is in no position to be impatient with the faults of others, for he knows himself well, and he knows how patient God has been with his own weaknesses. The habit of judging others'

---

[54] Ibid., no. 100, 190.

souls, however, could be a sign that someone does not really know himself or the God who loves us.

As St. Bernard of Clairvaux taught, "If you have eyes for the shortcomings of your neighbor and not for your own, no feeling of mercy will arise in you but rather indignation. You will be more ready to judge than to help, to crush in the spirit of anger than to instruct in the spirit of gentleness."[55] St. Bernard went on to explain how only the truly humble man will have compassion on his brothers' weaknesses: "The sound person feels not the sick one's pains, nor the well-fed the pangs of the hungry. It is fellow sufferers that readily feel compassion for the sick and the hungry ... You will never have real mercy for the failings of another until you know and realize that you have the same failings in your soul."[56] Pope Francis made a similar point: "The more conscious we are of our wretchedness and our sins, the more we experience the love and infinite mercy of God among us, and the more capable we are of looking upon the many 'wounded' we meet along the way with acceptance and mercy."[57]

> "You will never have real mercy for the failings of another until you know and realize that you have the same failings in your soul."
> —St. Bernard of Clairvaux

---

[55] St. Bernard of Clairvaux, *The Steps of Humility and Pride*, no. 13ff., in *Bernard of Clairvaux: A Lover Teaching the Way of Love*, ed. M. Basil Pennington (Hyde Park, New York: New City Press, 1997), 63.

[56] Ibid., no. 6, 63.

[57] Pope Francis, *The Name of God is Mercy*, 67.

Questions for Reflection/Discussion

1. How do you tend to respond when you notice someone's faults? Think about the people close to you. Are you quick to respond to their shortcomings with patience, gentleness, and mercy? Or do you tend to react with frustration, critical thoughts, or judgment? What can you do to cultivate a more compassionate heart?

2. How does God respond to our faults?

3. Why is it dangerous to condemn people when we happen to notice a certain fault of theirs—what might we not be seeing?

4. We saw how St. Catherine of Siena said judging others is "the devil's trap." How is this so?

5. Reflect on this statement from St. Bernard: "You will never have real mercy for the failings of another until you know and realize that you have the same failings in your soul." What does this mean? How does it inspire you to grow in compassion for others?

CONCLUSION

Conclusion

Should We Ever Talk About the
Elephant in the Room?

God has a mission for you. He wants every person you come in contact with to look up and see Jesus shining through you. And he has put certain people in your life for that very reason. It may be only through you that someone at work, or in your neighborhood, or in your family will encounter the merciful love of Jesus and the truth of his moral plan for our lives.

Think about the people in your life. There may be someone you know right now who is carrying a deep burden—shame over something they've done in the past or something they're struggling with now that they feel they cannot change. They don't know how much God loves them and wants to forgive them, help them, and heal them. Will you be Jesus to them?

Or there may be someone you know who is persisting in a certain sin—perhaps in their marriage, in their sexual lives, in the way they're treating someone, in how they spend their time, or in what they do on the weekends. Perhaps they've never been shown a better way to live life or heard a good explanation for why their actions might be wrong. God wants to lift them out of the superficial life they are living so they may experience deeper love, friendship, and happiness. Will you be Jesus to them?

Sadly, when God gives us opportunities to share his love and truth with others, many times we remain silent out of fear.

Fear of Conflict

Relativism creeps into the hearts of many good Christians. Out of fear of offending others, we rarely talk with our friends and family about the things that matter most in life. Relativism takes the most beautiful treasures of our Faith— Who is God? What is love? What is marriage? What is sex? What is man and woman?—and turns all these profound gems into elephants in the room. If we dare bring up, "What is life all about?" we're told by the culture, "Ssshh! You should never talk about those things with other people. You might offend them!"

As a result, we don't really encounter each other anymore. We're always side-stepping "hot-button" issues. Out of fear of rocking the boat, our interactions with our friends and family often are reduced to the superficial. Our conversations never rise above sports, movies, work, the news, and what's trending on social media. We might do a good job of avoiding conflict, but do we really love each other? Are we really sharing life together? We might coexist with these people, but deep down we know the relationships are shallow. Fake and artificial doesn't fulfill our heart's desire for real love and real unity.

> Are we avoiding certain topics with a friend because we're afraid and have no intention of ever talking about sensitive topics?

I hope this book has helped encourage you to be more authentic with the people in your life and given you some practical strategies of how to do that with greater courage and compassion. We all should strive to seek truth together with our relativistic friends as opposed to being the kind of people who shy away from meaningful conversations. Indeed, we ought to be able to have substantial discussions with people we disagree with, especially on the topics that are most important in life. I hope the book has given you some ideas of how to do that—not just in a more compassionate way, but with greater courage and love.

Silence with a Purpose

While we have an obligation to share the truth with others, in some situations, it may be prudent *not* to bring up certain moral topics with a friend. The person might not be ready right now. More time might be needed to build up trust. Certain hurts from the past might need to be healed first. Other more fundamental truths about God and life might need to be accepted before delving into this particular moral issue. There were times when Jesus chose to remain silent, and we too may face situations when choosing not to engage is the best option, at least for the present.

But many times it's not prudence that's driving our soft approaches with our relativistic friends. It's cowardice. We remain silent with a certain friend or family member simply because we're afraid. We're afraid of what it might cost us. We're afraid of potential awkwardness, tension, rejection, or failure. We don't know what to say, so we say nothing. Or maybe we just want to fit in. We want to be accepted and liked.

If we allow our fears to control us, however, we likely will subtly change our ideas about how much our friends need moral truth. For it's easier to change our ideas about the value of morality than it is to challenge our friends with the moral truth itself. So I tell myself, "Well, I might not agree with what they're doing, but I need to keep a good relationship with them. I want to keep peace. I want them to feel welcomed and accepted, so I just won't say anything. That way I won't offend them."

Here we must carefully examine our consciences: Are we avoiding certain topics with a friend because we love this person and want to share the Gospel with them eventually or because we're afraid, want to fit in, and have no intention of ever talking about sensitive topics? In other words, are we sincerely waiting for the right time and doing all we can spiritually and interpersonally on our end to prepare for that crucial conversation? Or is our "say nothing" approach just a cop-out so we don't have to do the work of evangelization with the people we claim to love?

One way to examine our true motives is to ask ourselves this question: Am I a thermometer or a thermostat in these relationships? A *thermometer* conforms to the environment around it. If it's hot in the room, the thermometer registers a higher temperature, and if it's cold the thermometer reading goes down. A *thermostat*, however, is not passive. It influences the world around it. It brings the temperature in the room to the appropriate level.

Consider your interactions with relativistic friends and family members. Are you a passive thermometer, always going along with what they do, talking about what they talk about, pretending everything is okay, and hiding your moral beliefs and faith as much as possible just so you can fit in and be accepted? A silent approach that is going nowhere and never offers a counter-cultural witness is not love. And it's certainly not evangelization.

Or are you more like a thermostat, intentionally trying to influence the world around you, to bring Jesus and his truth and love to the people God has placed in your life? If so, you might choose in some circumstances to avoid certain topics, but you're doing it out of love, not fear. In other words, you're sincerely seeking what is best for that person—not what is easier and more comfortable for yourself. You recognize now might not be the best time to address the issue head on, so you prudently choose not to bring it up. You are waiting for, hoping for, and, indeed, preparing the way for a time when the conversation is more likely to be fruitful. You remain silent in the present for the sake of evangelization in the future, not for the self-serving motive of fitting in.

> Evangelization is not about "us" versus "them" or about proving we're right and they're wrong.

Another way to evaluate your true motives is to consider whether you are striving to advance the ball down the field of evangelization with these people God has placed in your life. Are you praying for the person? Fasting for them? Asking God for opportunities to talk about the Faith with that person? Asking God to bring other good influences into their lives? Are you sincerely looking for opportunities to share the truth with your friend?

This, of course, doesn't mean that we show up at Thanksgiving dinner with the hammer of truth ready to pounce on your relatives about all their incorrect moral views and lifestyles. Evangelization is not about "us" versus "them" or about proving we're right and they're wrong. Evangelization, at heart, is all about love. We've encountered the love and mercy of Jesus. We've experience the joy that comes in following God's plan for our lives. We know how much of a difference Jesus has made in our lives and because we love our friends, we want to share him with them. As Pope Francis wrote, "If we have received the love which restores meaning to our lives, how can we fail to share that love with others?"[58]

One of the best ways to evaluate whether I'm a thermostat or a thermometer in my relationships is to ask: How much am I going out of the way to invest my life personally in these relationships? St. Paul gave people not just the Gospel but his very self (1 Thes 2:8). How about you? Do you truly accompany people in their lives? This is a crucial first step in evangelization, and it's something anyone who has encountered Christ can easily do. It entails getting to know people, serving them, listening to them, sharing in their hopes and fears, joys and sorrows, questions and doubts in life. People in the modern world rarely have friends with whom they can talk about what matters most in life and what's really going on inside them. Be that authentic friend to them. Be Jesus to them. If you do, you're likely to discover opportunities to share the Gospel. They might open up a bit about something personal. They might ask your thoughts on a certain matter. They might be moved by your example. They might even seek your advice on something someday. And that gives you the chance to share from your own experience how a certain Scripture passage or insight from the faith has made a difference in your life. But if we remain like passive thermometers—if we just go with the flow in our relationships, never really getting to know the people in our lives and never lifting our conversations above "How's work going?" or "Do you think the Broncos will win this year?" or "Have you seen this video on YouTube?"—then we are unlikely to make much of a difference in their lives.

Let's go back to the funeral exercise one last time. Are you living your relationships now the way you will be happy with

---

[58]   Pope Francis, *Evangelii Gaudium* ("The Joy of the Gospel"), 8.

at the end of your life? In those final days, are you going to wish you had fit in more or that you had shared your faith more with those you love? Don't let the relativistic culture silence your witness. Remember, God put certain people in your life for a reason. Will you let Jesus shine through you to them? Or will you let the pressures of relativism keep you from becoming the kind of person you want to be—a good friend, relative, neighbor, child of God—someone who truly had an impact on others' lives, someone who fulfilled the mission God had entrusted to him and someone who loved his brothers and sisters enough to share the truth with them.

POSTSCRIPT

Postscript

"What Is Truth?"

At a crucial moment on Good Friday, after Jesus said he came to bear witness to the truth, the Roman Governor Pontius Pilate sarcastically replied, "What is truth?" (Jn 18:38).

Objective truth—a truth that applies to everyone—was not important for Pilate. He knew what a real revolutionary looked like, and he quickly realized Jesus was not one of them. He knew the real reason the Jewish leaders were accusing Jesus was because of their envy (Mt 27:18). He knew that Jesus was innocent. But the truth of Jesus's innocence didn't matter. Pilate had his own truth: he needed to do what was most expedient for his career. Pilate felt the pressure from the Jewish leaders and feared that crowds might start to riot. And once the people began to threaten him, saying, "If you release this man, you are not Caesar's friend; every one who makes himself a king sets himself against Caesar" (Jn 19:12), it was more than Pilate could handle. The truth of Jesus's innocence didn't matter. All that mattered to Pilate was that his reputation with Caesar didn't get tarnished by these Jewish leaders' threats. So he let an innocent man die in order to protect his own interests.

That's what happens when we deny moral truth. When there is no moral standard guiding us, we selfishly do what we want no matter how it affects other people. Like Pilate, when faced with a choice between doing what is right and doing what we want, we sometimes just do what we want and say, "What is truth?" But for the Christian, this is not just an abstract, philosophical choice between truth and relativism. It's ultimately a very personal choice about Jesus. For truth is not just an idea. It's a Person, Jesus Christ. Jesus himself said, "I am the way, the truth, and the life" (Jn 14:6). And when we deny a moral truth, we ultimately are denying Jesus himself.

While this book comes from a Catholic view of morality, much of what we've discussed does not depend on Christian sources. As we've seen, a lot of the central themes (such as virtue, friendship, freedom, and love) can be appreciated and accepted by people of various faith traditions, backgrounds, and lifestyles. But in this final section, I will address a few other questions that are related more directly to the Christian Faith. Since these can be helpful for Christians to ponder as they answer their relativist friends' questions, I've included them here in this brief postscript.[59]

You believe God gave us a moral law. But my idea of God is different. I think God just wants us to live in peace and harmony and respect each other.

For many today, how one thinks about God and God's moral law is on par with how one thinks about favorite

---

[59] For a fuller treatment of these and other topics about God, the Bible, Jesus, the Church, and the Catholic Faith as a whole, see my more extensive work: Edward Sri, *Love Unveiled: The Catholic Faith Explained* (San Francisco: Ignatius Press, 2015).

flavors of ice cream. Some like chocolate. Others prefer vanilla. Still others like strawberry. Which one is better? It's just a matter of preference. But is God like that? Does God adapt to my personal taste? If, for example, I happen to think God is an old man with a white beard living in the clouds, does that make him so in reality? Or if I think God is the wind, or a spiritual energy, or a rainbow, do my ideas about him make him who he is?

We can ask the same questions about God and morality. Just because the Aztecs thought human sacrifice was okay, the Nazis thought the Holocaust was good, and most Americans think premarital sex is fine, does that automatically make God approve of such actions? Or what if I happen to think God doesn't mind if I live with my girlfriend, use contraception in my marriage, steal from my neighbor, or kidnap children? Would my personal opinions about how I think God looks at my life make him actually approve of all my actions?

In summary, do I make God?

The answer, of course, is no. Just because I happen to think God doesn't give a moral law doesn't mean he really is that way. I don't make God. God exists from all eternity. He is ultimate reality. He's the One who created us, not the other way around. He doesn't conform to our opinions about him. Rather, our ideas should conform to who he is. And if we want to know God as he *really* is, we should consider whether he has revealed himself to us. Because if he has, whatever my personal opinion may be about whether God revealed a moral law has little significance compared with what God actually said about the matter.

But how do you know what God has said? Surely you don't believe God actually communicates with us! The whole notion of God sending prophets, inspiring

biblical authors, and becoming man seems like fairy tales and ancient myths.

While the overwhelming majority of people believe in God, many do not believe he is involved in our world. He does not hear our prayers. He does not help us in our need. He does not perform miracles. If someone is not convinced God is personally involved in this world, then he certainly is not going to think God reveals himself through prophets, Jesus, the Scriptures, or the Church. God may have created the universe a long time ago, but he has been sitting back and watching us from a distance ever since.

But does this view of God make sense? Is it reasonable to say God *can't* reveal himself and interact in this world? First, God certainly has the *ability* to do so. He's the Creator of the universe, after all, and he surely has the ability to interact with the world he brought into existence. If a builder has the ability to construct a building, would it be logical to conclude that he does not have the ability to enter into the building he just built and work in it? Similarly, if God created the universe, would it be reasonable to say he doesn't have the ability to enter into the world he brought into existence? It simply doesn't make sense to say that it's *impossible* for God to interact in this world and reveal himself to his people.

And we can go a step further. It is quite fitting that he would do this. We need God's help to understand who he is and his plan for our lives. As the medieval theologian St. Thomas Aquinas taught, our finite minds cannot fully comprehend the infinite God on their own.[60] Many of us humans have a hard enough time wrapping our minds around difficult subjects such as biochemistry, calculus, and

---

[60] St. Thomas Aquinas, *Summa Theologica*, Ia.1.1.

astrophysics. How much harder it is to grasp the almighty, all-holy, infinite God! If God wants us to know him and love him, therefore, it is fitting that he would reveal himself to us. Indeed, Christians don't believe in an impersonal higher power who remains aloof and uninvolved. We believe in the God who is love (1 Jn 4:8). And if God is love, it is most fitting that he would lovingly seek us out and reveal himself to us, so that we could be united to him.

But God is too big to fit in any one religion. I think there are many different roads leading up the same mountain to God. It's arrogant to claim that your church has more truth than others.

This view might be understandable if all the roads between God and us were manmade—if religion was merely about man's search for God. But Christianity is more about God's search for us. Indeed, Christians would argue that a passive, detached, uninvolved God—a God who leaves us completely on our own to find our way to him—doesn't make sense. Christians believe in a God of love, a God who loves us so much he personally seeks us out, reveals himself to us, and even became one of us in Jesus, forging the road between God and man. In the words of Peter Kreeft, "There is no human way up the mountain, only a divine way down."[61]

If God loves us so much, doesn't it seem likely he would come to us and show us the best way to him? Kreeft goes on to challenge the popular "all roads are the same" mentality: "If God made the road, we must find out whether he made many or one. If he made only one, then the shoe is on the other foot: it is humility, not arrogance, to accept this one

---

[61] Peter Kreeft, *Fundamentals of the Faith* (San Francisco: Ignatius Press, 1988), 76.

road from God; and it is arrogance, not humility, to insist that our man-made roads are as good as God's God-made one."[62] We should, therefore, at least consider the possibility that God may have taken the effort to reveal himself to us and show us his plan for our lives. That's actually what Jesus claimed when he said he is "the way, the truth, and the life" (Jn 14:6). If Jesus is, in fact, the way to the Father, then that's something we should consider for our lives!

Jesus was a good man, but he's not God. He might have been a good teacher, but he's just one of many inspiring religious leaders from whom I can learn.

Actually, Jesus is remarkably unique. In other religions, the founder claimed to be a messenger sent from God or a teacher leading us to God. Muhammad claimed to be a prophet sent from Allah. Buddha taught a spiritual path to inner tranquility. Confucius offered principles for living a balanced life. But Jesus was different. He didn't just offer a way to God or teach truth about God. He said, "I am the way, the truth, and the life" (Jn 14:6). He didn't just tell people to believe in God. He called them to believe in *him*.

If we consider his life in his first century Jewish context, it's clear that Jesus claimed to be much more than a good man. He acted and spoke in the Person of God. For example, he claimed to forgive sins, which was something only God could do (Lk 5:20–21). He put the authority of his own interpretation of the Law (the Torah) on par with the authority of God himself, quoting the divinely given Torah and then saying, "But I say to you ... " (Mt 5:21–48). Indeed, Jesus asserted equality with God, saying, "I and the Father

---

[62] Ibid., 77.

are one" (Jn 10:30). His claim was so bold that the Jewish leaders accused him of blasphemy and prepared to stone him to death, saying, "You, being a man, make yourself God" (Jn 10:33). Jesus even used God's holy name "I AM" (in Hebrew, *Yahweh*) and applied it to himself, saying, "Before Abraham was, I am" (Jn 8:58–59). Once again, Jesus's hearers accused him of blasphemy and tried to stone him to death. It's clear Jesus didn't just claim to be a good man, moral teacher, or prophet. He claimed to be God.

But that claim is unsettling. Jesus's claim to divinity isn't something merely to be discussed in a theology course. It challenges each of us *personally*: If Jesus is God, then he has authority over my life. I'll have to follow him, and that might involve making changes in the way I live. I think that's why many people say, "Jesus was just a good man." If someone doesn't want to reject Jesus outright, but at the same time he doesn't want to change, it's easier to simply say Jesus is a good man. That way, he can ease his conscience by picking and choosing what he likes from Jesus's teachings without actually having to follow him. He can continue living however he wants without having to look Jesus in the eye and say, "I reject you."

But the real Jesus doesn't give us that option. He challenges us to make a very personal choice about him. Either Jesus is who he said he was, or he isn't. He either is Lord of all, or he is not Lord at all. The one thing we can't say is that Jesus was merely a good man. For if Jesus claimed to be God and wasn't, he was either a crazy man who was very confused about his identity or he was a wicked man who has deceived millions and millions of people. We might feel sorry for Jesus if he were crazy. Or we might fight against him if he were a liar. But, as the popular twentieth-century Christian writer C. S. Lewis explained, it does not make sense to say

Jesus was just a good man.[63] The real Jesus won't let us get away with that.

So who will you say Jesus is? Will you welcome him as the Lord of your life?

I'm okay with Jesus. But why do I need a church?

When Jesus described the community of his followers, he used the word "church" or *ekklesia*—a Greek word derived from *ek kalein*, which means "to call out of." It's an important word in the Bible used to describe the people of Israel, whom God *called out* of slavery in Egypt. God called them out of slavery and established them as his Chosen People. Jesus chose that particular word to describe his followers. Through his Church, Jesus *calls us out* of ourselves—he calls us out of our limited perspectives and our selfishness. He calls us out of our slavery to sin.

A danger in seeking God all on our own, apart from the Church, is that we tend to make God in our own image and likeness. We tend to build a spirituality and morality that suits our comforts and interests—one that justifies the way we are currently living and that doesn't challenge us to grow. In other words, it's easier to make up my own spirituality than it is to accept a Church that calls me on to greater love, generosity, sacrifice, and responsibility. In the world of being spiritual but not religious, I can create my own values and make myself my own pope in my own religion, the Church of Me.

More trustworthy than basing my life on my own made-up values is following the standards of Jesus Christ. More

---

[63] C. S. Lewis, *Mere Christianity*, 54-55.

trustworthy than the Church of Me is the Church Jesus actually founded. God became man in Jesus Christ, whose words and deeds represent the fullness of God's unveiling of himself and his plan for our lives. Jesus entrusted that revelation to his Apostles, to whom he gave authority to teach in his name (Mt 10:1–8; Mt 28:18–20). Jesus said to them, "He who hears you hears me, and he who rejects you rejects me" (Lk 10:16). Notice how closely Jesus identified himself with his Apostles. To the extent that someone in the first century received the teaching authority of Peter, Andrew, John, and the other Apostles, they were receiving Christ. But to reject the authority of the Apostles was not just a rejection of these men. It was a rejection of Christ himself. Jesus promised to work through the Apostles and gave them authority to teach his truth, and that authority was passed on from the Apostles to their successors throughout the ages. The bishops today stand in that long line of apostolic succession and, in union with the Bishop of Rome, the Pope, they pass on the truth of Jesus Christ; and with the guidance of the Holy Spirit they faithfully apply his teachings to our present day situations.[64]

But I'm afraid to say a certain behavior is immoral. I don't want to rock the boat with my friends and family. So I'll just say it's wrong for me, but, if others want to do it, then that's okay for them.

For the Christian, standing up for moral truth comes down to this fundamental question: Who do you say Jesus is? Do you treat Jesus merely as a good man from whose teaching

---

[64] For more on the Church, see my *Love Unveiled* (San Francisco: Ignatius Press, 2015), 117-136.

you can pick and choose what you want to accept and what you want to set aside? Or do you believe Jesus really is who he said he is: not just a good man, but the divine Son of God whose entire teachings should shape our entire lives? Jesus himself said it's not enough to call him Lord without doing anything about it. He wants us to welcome him as Lord over our lives and follow his teachings: "Why do you call me 'Lord, Lord,' and not do what I tell you?" (Lk 6:46). He is a good Lord, the one who made us, who knows what is best for us and wants our happiness more than we do. Why wouldn't you trust him with your life?

Many of us will have questions about specific moral issues—why does the Church teach *X*? What is wrong with *Y*? Why can't we do *Z*? That's normal. Our faith is always seeking deeper understanding. We should take our questions to good, trusted friends, teachers, priests, and resources that can help answer our questions. And we certainly should take our questions about morality to God himself in prayer. Like the man in the Gospel story, we can say, "Lord, 'I believe; Help my unbelief!'" (cf. Mk 9:24).

But the fundamental issue remains: Do we trust Jesus? To the extent that a Christian embraces Jesus's moral teachings, he is saying yes to Jesus himself. But think about what happens when we embrace relativism, even the conditional "for me" forms of relativism we've considered in this book ("abortion is wrong *for me*," "pre-marital sex is wrong *for me*"). Insofar as we embrace relativism and deny moral truth, to that extent we deny Jesus himself. Remember, God loved us so much that he took the trouble to reveal himself to us and give us the Church to show us the moral law as the pathway to our happiness. Especially in our troubled era, Christ and his Church are like a sure anchor keeping us grounded in reality, and keeping us from being "carried about with every wind of doctrine, by the cunning of men, by their craftiness in deceitful wiles" (Eph 4:14).

Don't brush aside Jesus's teachings just because you want to fit in—because you're afraid of holding a controversial position, of being labeled judgmental, of rocking the boat with friends and family, or of saying what your coworker, brother, or aunt is doing is wrong. We should always talk about morality with humility, gentleness, mercy, and love—in the right way and at the right time. But will you stand up for moral truth? Or will you remain silent just because you want to be accepted by your peers? Will you let your fear of conflict keep you from being faithful to Our Lord, Jesus Christ? In other words, will you stand with Pilate, saying "What is truth"? or will you stand with Jesus, the Son of God, who not only came to reveal the truth, but who in his very being *is* the way, the truth, and the life?

Acknowledgments

I am grateful for the many colleagues, students and missionaries at Benedictine College, Augustine Institute and the Fellowship of Catholic University Students (FOCUS) with whom I have discussed the topic of moral relativism throughout the years. Their questions, comments and insights have greatly enriched my teaching on the topic and have, no doubt, left their mark on the pages of this work. I'm thankful for feedback from Ben Akers, Chris Blum, Curtis Mitch, Lucas Pollice, John Sehorn and Jared Staudt on certain sections of the book. Special thanks also goes to John Bishop and Megan O'Neil for their very helpful review of the manuscript, to the Augustine Institute students who studied the topic with me in the months in which the writing took place and to the young adults in Denver who participated in the filming of the accompanying video series for adult faith formation and small group studies. I express my gratitude to the video production, editorial, graphic design and marketing teams at the Augustine Institute for pouring their hearts into helping bring this project to fruition. Finally, I am indebted to my wife, Elizabeth, for her encouraging me to do this book and for her constant prayers and support throughout its writing.